# THE SUPREME COURT
# OF THE UNITED STATES

# THE SUPREME COURT
# OF THE UNITED STATES

## ITS FOUNDATION, METHODS AND
## ACHIEVEMENTS: AN INTERPRETATION

BY
### CHARLES EVANS HUGHES

## COLUMBIA UNIVERSITY PRESS
NEW YORK AND LONDON

The lectures in this book were originally delivered as part of the Columbia University Lectures under the George Blumenthal Foundation.

# CONTENTS

# FOREWORD

It would be futile to attempt in this brief course of lectures to review the history of the Supreme Court of the United States. What had been lacking in narratives of this sort, in order fully to understand the relation of the Court to the history of our country, has recently been supplied in Mr. Warren's comprehensive volumes. For the student of constitutional law nothing would suffice but a thorough-going analysis of many decisions and an impressionistic treatment would be but vexation. My endeavor will be simply to aid to some extent in the interpretation of an institution which despite its constant and unique service is a mystery, I fear, to most of our people; to assist those, who are not aiming to become legal scholars, to understand something of its origin, of the principles that govern it, of its methods and of the important results of its work. Even with this limitation, much that I should like to say must be omitted.

# I

## Introduction — Foundations

The Supreme Court of the United States is distinctly American in conception and function, and owes little to prior judicial institutions aside from the Anglo-Saxon tradition of law and judicial processes. In considering the historical background of the Court, it does not aid much to review experiences in other lands.

A Federal judiciary was an essential part of the conception of a national government of a Federal type. Such a government must have its legislature and a court to interpret legislation. State courts would be bound by Federal laws and would have to apply them, but final interpretation of such laws could not be left to a State tribunal, much less to the tribunals of a number of States whose judgments might not agree. The proposed Federal government was of necessity, in view of the existence of the States and of the sentiment which supported them as autonomous within their spheres, to be one of limited powers. To establish such a government was the purpose of a written constitution. The framers of the Constitution intended that the Federal government to be set up should act directly upon the individual citizen and not simply upon the States. This was the essence of its national character. If there was to be a written constitution defining, and thus limiting, Federal powers, and these definitions were to have the force of constitutional or supreme law, it would be essential that the tribunal which interpreted and applied Federal law should recognize and apply the limits of both Federal and State authority. And as that government acted upon the individual citizen, he was deemed to be entitled to invoke its limitations. Thus, in the most natural way, as the result of the creation of Federal law under a written constitution conferring limited powers, the Supreme Court of the United States came into being with its unique function. That court maintains the balance between State and Nation through the maintenance of the rights and duties of individuals.

The men who sat in the Federal Convention of 1787 had political ideals but these did not run away with their practical judgment. The appreciation of definite exigencies had slowly developed a national consciousness. The character of the tribunal set up was due not to experiences abroad or to the wisdom of other peoples, but to convictions which had become deep-seated as a result of the experiences of the Colonies and of the States that succeeded them. The common law of England, variously interpreted in the courts of the Colonies, was the basis of their jurisprudence. It was fitted to their needs both by their legislatures and by judicial decisions. Appeals generally lay from the courts to the legislative assemblies and finally to the King in Council, this resort to the Crown, thoroughly established long before the Revolution, being deemed, as Story remarks,[1] a protection rather than a grievance. The colonial judges for the most part were appointed by the Crown or its representatives, the Governors. In Connecticut and Rhode Island the appointment was made by the legislature. As a rule, the bench was not learned and the selection of judges was largely determined by politics or favor. Of the judges of the first superior court in Massachusetts, none were lawyers.[2] The growth of the Colonies and the increase of judicial work favored the development of judicial tribunals. But nowhere in the Colonies was there a real supreme court.[3] In New York, the decisions of the court so-called were subject to review by the Governor and Council.[4]

In establishing their constitutions, the States improved to some extent the existing judicial systems, and the highest court of the State became the court of last resort in place of the King in Council. The lawyers of that formative period were, as they had been in the Colonies, in advance of the institutions of the law which were but rudimentary. We may recall what Chancellor Kent said many years later as to conditions in New York: "The progress of jurisprudence was nothing in this State (New York) prior to the year 1793. There were no deci-

[1] *Story on the Constitution*, Sec. 176.

[2] Baldwin, *The American Judiciary*, 9.

[3] Baldwin, *op. cit*, 10.

[4] Lincoln, *Constitutional History of New York*, vol. i, 39, 40; Hunt, *Life of Edward Livingston*, 26.

sions of any of the courts published. There were none that contained any investigation".[5]

With these defects in the local administration of justice, what was the situation as to controversies which transcended local interests? There had been a fierce contest with respect to the powers given to admiralty courts in the pre-revolutionary period. With the beginning of hostilities, questions of prize assumed large importance. In November, 1775, Washington asked the Continental Congress — "Should not a court be established by authority of Congress, to take cognizance of prizes made by the Continental vessels?"[6] The Congress responded with recommendations to the State legislatures to establish jurisdiction in cases of capture with appeal to Congress or its appointees.[7] The States established the jurisdiction with varying methods. Some granted liberally, others restricted, the appeal to Congress. On the first appeal from the Admiralty Court of Pennsylvania in the case of the "Thistle" a special committee was appointed and on its report the decree condemning the vessel as a prize was reversed.[8] Later, a Standing Committee of the Congress was appointed to hear and determine appeals in admiralty. The members of the committee were men of high distinction.[9] In the case of the sloop "Active," the Admiralty Court of Pennsylvania,

[5] *Memoirs and Letters*, 58, 59.

[6] Sparks, *Life and Letters of Washington*, vol. iii, 154, 155.

[7] *Journals of Congress*, vol. i, 183, 184.

[8] *Id.*, vol. i, pp. 470, 499.

[9] *Id.*, vol. ii, 28, 119, 287, 338.

which had been reversed by the Standing Committee of the Continental Congress, refused to recognize the decision and the resistance was effective, the Congress contenting itself with a strong statement in defense of its authority without attempting to enforce it.[10]

Meanwhile, in the Articles of Confederation submitted by the Congress in November, 1777, and finally ratified in 1781, it was provided (Ninth Article) that the United States in Congress assembled should have the sole and exclusive right and power "of establishing rules for deciding in all cases what captures on land or water shall be legal"; of appointing courts for the trial of piracies and felonies committed on the high seas; and of establishing courts for receiving and determining finally appeals in all cases of capture. The United States in Congress was to "be the last resort on appeal in all disputes * * * between * * * states concerning boundary, jurisdiction, or any other cause whatever"; also in "all controversies concerning the private right of soil claimed under different grants of two or more states." Before the completion of the ratification of the Articles, the Congress resolved (1780) to establish a Court of Appeals in cases of capture.[11] Altogether, 117 cases of prize were decided by the Standing Committee on Appeals and the Court of Appeals.[12] In

10 See *United States v. Judge Peters, 5 Cranch,* 115.

11 *Journals of Congress,* Vol. III, 425.

12 J. C. Bancroft Davis, 131 U. S. Appendix, XIX, XXXV, et seq.

1795, the Supreme Court of the United States, speaking through Justice Paterson, who sat in the Constitutional Convention, sustained the authority of the Continental Congress, both before and after the Articles of Confederation, to establish the Court of Appeals in cases of capture.[13] He said, — describing the powers of that Congress —

"The powers of Congress were revolutionary in their nature, arising out of events, adequate to every national emergency, and co-extensive with the object to be attained. Congress was the general, supreme, and controlling council of the nation, the centre of union, the centre of force, and the sun of the political system. To determine what their powers were, we must enquire what powers they exercised. Congress raised armies, fitted out a navy, and prescribed rules for their government: Congress conducted all military operations both by land and sea: Congress emitted bills of credit, received and sent ambassadors, and made treaties: Congress commissioned privateers to cruize against the enemy, directed what vessels should be liable to capture, and prescribed rules for the distribution of prizes. These high acts of sovereignty were submitted to, acquiesced in, and approved of, by the people of America. In Congress were vested, because by Congress were exercised with the approbation of the people, the rights and powers of war and peace. In every government, whether it consists of many states, or of a few, or whether it be of a federal or

[13] *Penhallow v. Doane,* 3 Dallas, 54.

consolidated nature, there must be a supreme power or will; the rights of war and peace are component parts of this supremacy, and incidental thereto is the question of prize. The question of prize grows out of the nature of the thing. If it be asked, in whom, during our revolution war, was lodged, and by whom was exercised this supreme authority? No one will hesitate for an answer. It was lodged in, and exercised by, Congress; it was there, or nowhere; the states individually did not, and, with safety, could not exercise it.'' [14]

It has been pointed out that this practice in cases of capture before the Constitution, although in a limited field, familiarized "the public mind with the complete idea of a superior judicature, exercised by federal courts.'' [15] While certain controversies between States were settled by agreement during the time that the Articles of Confederation were in force, there was one case actually decided under the provision of the Articles. The Congress directed Connecticut and Pennsylvania to appoint by joint consent commissioners or judges to determine the Wyoming controversy. This was done in 1782 and judgment was pronounced in favor of Pennsylvania.[16] This was the only decision of a controversy between States under the Confederation.[17]

The experience under the Confederation amply

[14] *Id.*, 80.

[15] Jameson, *Papers of American Historical Association*, Vol. 3, p. 392, 1887-88.

[16] J. C. Bancroft Davis, 131 U. S. Appendix, 1, LVII.

[17] Carson, *Supreme Court of the United States*, Vol. I, 69-72.

demonstrated the necessity of defining and firmly establishing the Federal judicial power. The people for the most part had no love for government as such. The acquiescence in the authority of Congress under the Confederation, eloquently portrayed by Justice Paterson in the *Penhallow* case, from which I have quoted, was far from being as conspicuous as his language indicates. "We are fast verging to anarchy and confusion," [18] said Washington. "Requisitions are actually little better than a jest & a by word throughout the land. If you tell the Legislatures they have violated the Treaty of Peace, & invaded the prerogatives of the confederacy they will laugh in your face * * * " [19] Washington felt that "virtue * * * has, in a great degree, taken its departure from us: & the want of disposition to do justice is the source of the national embarrassments * * *." [20] A strange atmosphere in which to set up the most important and successful of judicial institutions! But there was clear thinking as to national needs and it was precisely because of these conditions that the leaders emphasized the importance of an adequate Federal judiciary. Hamilton thought that "the want of a judiciary power" was the crowning defect of the Confederation.[21] Madison wrote to Washington in April, 1787: "The national supremacy ought also to be extended as I con-

---

[18] Washington to Madison, Nov. 5, 1786, *Documentary History of the Constitution of the United States,* Vol. IV, 34.

[19] Washington to Jay, Aug. 1, 1786, *Id.,* Vol. IV, 20.

[20] Washington to Jay, May 18, 1786, *Id.,* Vol. IV, 16.

[21] *Federalist,* XXII, Vol. 11, p. 176.

ceive to the Judiciary departments * * * It seems at least necessary that the oaths of the Judges should include a fidelity to the general as well as local constitution, and that an appeal should lie to some national tribunals in all cases to which foreigners or inhabitants of other States may be parties. The admiralty jurisdiction seems to fall entirely within the purview of the national Government." [22] Madison in his later correspondence was careful to explain "that the term national applied to the contemplated Government, in the early stage of the Convention" was not equivalent to "unlimited" or "consolidated." He used the term in contradistinction, not to a limited government, but to one similar to that of the Confederation. As the latter operated within the extent of its authority through requisitions on the confederated States and rested on the sanction of the state legislatures, the Government to take its place was to operate within the extent of its powers directly and coercively on individuals and to receive the higher sanction of the people of the States. The term "national" was used because there was "no technical or appropriate denomination applicable to the new and unique System." [23] It was not meant to express "the *extent* of power, but the *mode* of *its operation* * * * " [24]

As the larger number of the members of the Federal Convention, including those enjoying the highest

[22] Madison to Washington, April 16, 1787, *Doc. Hist. Constitution,* Vol. IV, 118.

[23] Madison to Stephenson, March 25, 1826, *Id.,* Vol. V, 333.

[24] Madison to Cooper, Dec. 26, 1826, *Id.,* Vol. V, 339.

prestige because of their learning, ability and public service, favored a strong national government in this sense, it was natural that there should have been but little question as to the necessity of having a national judiciary. Its creation was a part of the conception of the division of powers. The Randolph or Virginia plan presented to the Convention on May 29, 1787, proposed that "a National Judiciary be established to consist of one or more supreme tribunals, and of inferior tribunals to be chosen by the National Legislature * * *."[25] By the Pinckney plan, submitted on the same day, the Legislature of the United States was to establish such courts of Law, Equity and Admiralty as shall be necessary, and one of these courts was to be termed "the Supreme Court."[26] The Paterson plan, presented to the Convention on June fifteenth provided that "a federal Judiciary be established, to consist of a supreme Tribunal * * *."[27] Hamilton's proposal a few days later was that "the Supreme Judicial Authority of the United States" should be vested in a number of judges.[28]

With this measure of agreement, the Convention proceeded to the consideration of the organization of the judicial department. How many courts should there be? How should the judges be appointed? What should be their tenure? What should be the extent of jurisdiction? The Convention was peculiarly fitted to deal with these questions. Of its

[25] *Doc. Hist. Const.*, Vol. III, 19.
[26] *Id.*, Vol. I, 319.
[27] *Id.*, Vol. I, 324.
[28] *Id.*, Vol. I, 328.

fifty-five members, there were thirty-one lawyers, equipped not only with the technical learning of their profession but with a broad experience in practical affairs which gave them a seasoned judgment and the vision of statesmen. Four had studied in the Inner Temple, five in the Middle Temple, ten had been State judges, seven had been selected as judges to determine controversies between the States. Thirty-nine members of the Convention had served in the Continental Congress. Eight had taken part in the formulation of State constitutions. They were well qualified for every part of their task, and especially for the creation of the judicial institutions essential to the national life.

The Convention quickly determined on "one supreme tribunal," instead of one or more supreme tribunals as originally proposed in the Randolph plan. The provision as reported by the Committee on Detail on August sixth was as follows: "The Judicial Power of the United States shall be vested in one Supreme Court, and in such inferior Courts as shall, when necessary, from time to time, be constituted by the Legislature of the United States." [29] This is substantially the provision finally adopted with the substitution of "the Congress" for "the Legislature of the United States."

Serious questions were raised as to the method of appointing judges. How was the ideal of the separation of powers to be reconciled with practical exigencies? Despite the emphatic terms in which

[29] *Id.*, Vol. III, 454.

the political maxim had been laid down by the States, Madison found "not a single instance in which the several departments of power have been kept absolutely separate and distinct." [30] Jefferson in his "Notes on Virginia" observed that the legislature had in many instances "decided rights which should have been left to judiciary controversy." [31] Rhode Island and Connecticut had long refused to recognize the principle of division of powers; in Connecticut, the legislature had been "in the uniform, uninterrupted, habit of exercising a general superintending power over its courts of law, by granting new trials." [32] After a careful review of State practice, Madison concluded that "the legislative department is everywhere extending the sphere of its activity, and drawing all power into its impetuous vortex." [33]

In many States, the legislature appointed the judges directly, and, notwithstanding the devotion to the doctrine of Montesquieu, it is not surprising that in the Federal Convention the Virginia plan should have proposed that the national legislature should appoint the judges of the Supreme Court. The Paterson plan provided for appointment by the Executive. James Wilson opposed appointment by the legislature. He said: "Experience showed the impropriety of such appointments by numerous

[30] *Federalist*, XLVII, Vol. 12, p. 18.
[31] *Notes on Virginia*, 3d Am. Edi., p. 175,   Query XIII.
[32] *Calder v. Bull*, 3 Dallas, 386, 398.
[33] *Federalist*, XLVIII, Vol. 12, p. 25.

bodies. Intrigue, partiality and concealment were the necessary consequences. A principal reason for unity in the Executive was that officers might be appointed by a single, responsible person." [34] Dr. Franklin observed that two modes of choice had been mentioned, to-wit, by the Legislature and by the Executive. He wished that other modes might be suggested, "it being a point of great moment." [35] Madison objected to appointment by the *whole* legislature. "Many of them were incompetent judges of the requisite qualifications. * * * The candidate who was present, who had displayed a talent for business in the legislative field, who had perhaps assisted ignorant members in business of their own, or of their Constituents, or used other winning means, would without any of the essential qualifications for an expositor of the laws prevail over a competitor not having these recommendations, but possessed of every necessary accomplishment." Madison proposed appointment by the Senate "as a less numerous & more select body"; or, as he had said earlier, as "sufficiently stable and independent." [36] This was adopted by the Committee of the Whole in their report on the Randolph plan and was embraced in the report of the Committee on Detail. Meanwhile it had been suggested, with reference to the practice in Massachusetts, that the judges be appointed by

[34] *Doc. Hist. Constitution,* Vol. III, 62.

[35] *Id.,* Vol. III, 63.

[36] *Id.,* Vol. III, 118, 64.

the Executive, with the advice and consent of the Senate, and this proposal was finally adopted.[37]

On the question of tenure there was a surprising lack of disagreement. All the plans agreed on the point that the judges should hold office during good behavior and that they should receive a fixed compensation which should be neither increased nor diminished while they were in office. This proposal was adopted by the Convention with the elimination of the prohibition of an increase in compensation. Gouverneur Morris thought "the Legislature ought to be at liberty to increase salaries as circumstances might require, and that this would not create any improper dependence in the Judges." Dr. Franklin in approving this change observed that "money may not only become plentier, but the business of the department may increase as the Country becomes more populous." Madison opposed, fearing that whenever an increase is wished by the judges they might have an "undue complaisance" towards the legislature. He thought that if leading members of the legislature happened to be parties to suits in court "at such a crisis" the judges would be "in a situation which ought not be suffered * * *."[38] This illustrates what groundless fears even the wisest may entertain. The withholding of authority to increase compensation in the case of judicial officers appointed virtually for life would have caused

[37] *Id.*, Vol. III, 363; See *Constitution of Massachusetts* (1780). Chap. II, Sec. I, Art 9.

[38] *Doc. Hist. Constitution*, Vol. III, 367.

grave injustice and such modest increases as from time to time have been allowed have not been a cause of embarrassment.

The unanimity of view that the tenure of the judges should be during good behavior was due to the grave importance attached to their independence. That judicial commissions should run during good behavior was a reform secured by the Long Parliament in England and such commissions had been granted in the colonies. The Declaration of Independence set forth the grievance that George III had changed this and had made judges dependent upon his will alone for the tenure of their offices and the amount and payment of their salaries. The constitutions of a number of the States had provided that judges should hold office during good behavior. This was true in Massachusetts, Virginia, the Carolinas, Maryland, Delaware and in New York, save that in New York the judges had to retire at the age of sixty. In some States there were short terms, seven years in Pennsylvania and New Jersey. In Georgia, Connecticut and Rhode Island the judges were chosen annually.[39] The prevailing opinion in the Federal Convention thus had abundant support in practice. It was thought to be plain that justice under the new constitution, with its novel demands upon ability and impartiality in maintaining the balance of a unique system of government, would fare better by having

[39] Thorpe, *Charters and Constitutions*, pp. 531, 564, 784, 1689, 1905, 2596, 2634, 2791, 3216, 3246, 3817; Carpenter, *Judicial Tenure in the United States,* 4.

the judges independent than by subjecting them to the political control incident to a shorter term. The framers of the Constitution were intent on protection against legislative encroachments, and put their trust in the learning, ability, and conscientiousness of the judges rather than in any device of political mastery. In the Federalist, urging support of this provision of the Constitution, Hamilton argued that "the complete independence of the courts of justice is peculiarly essential in a limited Constitution," that is, in "one which contains certain specified exceptions to the legislative authority." He pointed out, and this was before ratification, that "limitations of this kind can be preserved in practice no other way than through the medium of courts of justice, whose duty it must be to declare all acts contrary to the manifest tenor of the Constitution void. Without this, all the reservations of particular rights or privileges would amount to nothing." It was urged that "periodical appointment" of judges, "however regulated or by whomsoever made, would, in some way or other, be fatal to their necessary independence." [40]

The policy which generally has been adopted by the States as to the selection and tenure of judicial officers has afforded a strikng contrast to the policy thus established in the Federal government. Popular elections for short terms have come to be the general rule. The administration of justice in the States gave many grounds for dissatisfaction. De-

[40] *Federalist*, LXXVIII, vol. 12, pp. 257, 263.

lays and abuses demanded correction, and the idea
that the courts were not sufficiently democratic became dominant.  In comparing the advantages of the
methods of choice, — election and appointment, —
it is easy to fall into extravagant statement by attaching undue importance to theoretical considerations.  From our experience it may be said that the
evils of political manipulation incident to popular
elections have been most in evidence in relation to
the lower courts, and especially in great cities, and
have been counteracted most effectively in connection with appellate tribunals.  In the quality of the
judges, the general satisfaction of the public with
their work, and the prestige of the court, an impartial observer of the highest courts of Massachusetts,
New Jersey, New York and Wisconsin, for example,
would find it difficult to prefer one over another although in Massachusetts and New Jersey the judges
are appointed and in New York and Wisconsin
they are elected.  The active interest of the most
thoughtful and intelligent citizens, and of the most
public-spirited members of the bar, increases with
the realization of the importance of the choice, and
hence there has been greater care in selecting, by
either method, the judges of the highest courts.

There are special considerations in the case of the
Supreme Court of the United States, and these have
been recognized when proposals for a change in the
method of selection have been made.  The vastness
of the country, the enormous population, the ines-
capable difficulties in the choice of President, the

opportunities for political intrigue that would exist in the nomination of judges by national party conventions, are cogent reasons for the continuance of the present method which has even more to be said for it now than it had in 1787. Qualifications for judicial office, learning, ability, integrity, independence, remain the same. What is the method that gives the best promise of obtaining judges of that sort for the highest tribunal of the nation? It would seem that there is no better way than to have the President nominate, and the Senate consent, with public attention focused on both acts.

As to tenure, aside from the question of retirement for age, to which I shall refer later, so much is to be said for the experience gained on the bench; so great is the importance of freedom from political interference, that one may conclude that probably more would be lost than could be gained by a change. Reflection upon the character and service of the judges who have sat for many years in the Supreme Court gives weight to this view. And yet I would not over-emphasize the point, for experience of the States having elections for definite terms has shown how strong is the demand for the continuance in office of good judges of the highest courts. Thus, in New York, under the pressure of the bar and the sound opinion of the community, both political parties have frequently co-operated in the renomination of judges, so that the average length of the service of judges of the Court of Appeals in that State compares favorably with that of the justices of the

Supreme Court of the United States. But in connection with the latter, we are spared recurring
political demands and, what is most important, the
justices of the Supreme Court dealing so largely
with constitutional questions of the gravest sort
may address themselves to their work with freedom
from anxiety as to their future and unembarrassed
by suspicion as to their motives. Cases involving
serious differences of opinion must be decided and,
whatever the decision where popular interest is keen,
there is sure to be a measure of disappointment.

The Federal judges were made subject to impeachment, as other civil officers of the United States, for
"Treason, Bribery or other high Crimes and Misdemeanors." [41] According to the weight of opinion,
impeachable offenses include, not merely acts that
are indictable, but serious misbehavior which may be
considered as coming within the category of high
crimes and misdemeanors. Only one Justice of the
Supreme Court has been impeached — Samuel
Chase, who was acquitted in 1805. A different procedure is removal upon address. The proposal that
the Federal judges should be removable by the Executive on the application of the Senate and House
was voted down in the Federal Convention. Gouverneur Morris thought it inconsistent that the judges
should hold their offices during good behavior and be
removable without a trial, and this was the pre-
ponderant opinion in the Convention.[42] In a num-

[41] *Constitution*, Art. II, Sec. 4.
[42] *Doc. Hist. Constitution*, Vol. III, 624.

ber of the State constitutions provision was made
for removal of judges upon address, following the
English example. This procedure, however, has
generally fallen into disuse. Legislative control of
judges is not desired and popular control has been
sought in the States through elections and short
terms. That remedy not being available under the
Federal Constitution, the importance of a power of
removal, as distinguished from impeachment, has
been urged strongly. There have been several
efforts, beginning with the bitter opposition to the
Federal judiciary in Jefferson's administration, to
introduce such a provision into the Federal Constitution, but these have been unsuccessful. In recent
years, confidence in the efficacy of the impeachment
process has been increased, the breadth of the jurisdiction being indicated in the case of Judge Archbald of the Federal Circuit Court (1913).[43] Long experience gives a practical answer to proposals for
the removal or recall of justices of the Supreme
Court. The high standards of integrity exemplified
by its members justifies the conclusion that the method of appointment, the dignity of the office, and the
force of public opinion have proved to be adequate
guaranties against breaches of duty which could be
regarded as warranting removal, and that the demand for change, under the guise of proceedings to
remove or recall, has been motivated by the desire
to obtain a political control of decisions, a question

[43] *Sen. Doc. 1140*, 62d Cong. 3d Sess. Judge Archbald was designated a member of the Commerce Court.

which goes not simply to the procedure for getting rid of an unfit judge, but rather to the character and value of the judicial institution itself and especially to the possession by the Supreme Court of the power to pass upon the constitutional validity of legislation. If the Supreme Court is to continue to perform this function, it would seem to be clear that the purpose of securing independent and impartial decisions in a non-political atmosphere would be made more difficult of accomplishment if such decisions, directly or indirectly, were subjected to political review.

In dealing with the question of the jurisdiction of the Supreme Court, the Federal Convention had certain obvious requirements which inhered in the establishment of a national government. On certain categories of jurisdiction, there was early agreement; that is, with respect to cases arising "under laws passed by the Legislature of the United States; to all cases affecting Ambassadors, other Public Ministers and Consuls; to the trial of impeachments of Officers of the United States; to all cases of Admiralty and maritime jurisdiction; to controversies between two or more States, (except such as shall regard Territory or Jurisdiction) between a State and Citizens of another State, between Citizens of different States, and between a State or the Citizens thereof and foreign States, citizens or subjects." [44] To these were added cases arising under treaties.

It was William Samuel Johnson, already chosen

[44] *Doc. Hist. Constitution*, Vol. III, 454.

President of Columbia College, who made the important proposal to insert the words "this Constitution," so that the jurisdiction should explicitly extend to cases arising under "this Constitution" as well as to cases arising under the laws of the United States. Madison expressed the doubt whether it would not be going too far "to extend the jurisdiction of the court generally to cases arising Under the Constitution, & whether it ought not be limited to cases of a Judiciary Nature." But Dr. Johnson's motion was passed unanimously, "it being generally supposed that the jurisdiction was constructively limited to cases of a Judiciary Nature." [45]

There were special questions: What should be the jurisdiction in cases of impeachment of civil officers? At first, while the House was to have the sole power of impeachment, the trial of impeachments was to be part of the original jurisdiction of the Supreme Court, but this was abandoned in favor of trial by the Senate, with the Chief Justice presiding in case of impeachment of the President. Then there was the question of controversies between the States. Following the general plan of the Ninth Article of the Articles of Confederation, it was proposed, and included in the report of the Committee on Detail, that in case of controversies between the States respecting jurisdiction or territory, the Senate on receiving a memorandum from a State and application for a hearing should give notice to the other State and assign a day for appearance. The agents of the

[45] *Id.*, Vo.' III, 626.

States were to appoint judges to constitute a court and if they could not agree the Senate was to name a panel from which the judges were to be chosen. The judgment of the Court thus constituted was to be final and conclusive. Controversies concerning lands claimed under different grants of two or more States were to be determined in a similar manner.[46]

Perhaps in no instance was the wisdom of the Convention better shown than in discarding this plausible proposal, which had the sanction of precedent, for creating what would be virtually arbitral tribunals to be set up after the controversies had arisen, with all the difficulties of establishing satisfactory tribunals in the heat of the dispute and with the disadvantage of impermanence. In the debate it was pointed out that such a provision was no longer necessary now that a national judiciary was to be established. But there were serious doubts. "The Judges might be connected with the States being parties." The provision was finally struck out and controversies between the States regarding territory or jurisdiction as well as other controversies between the States were confided to the jurisdiction of the Supreme Court, together with controversies between citizens of the same States claiming lands under grants of different States.

The jurisdiction of the Supreme Court is both original and appellate. The Convention restricted the *original* jurisdiction of the Supreme Court to all cases affecting ambassadors, other public ministers and

[46] *Id.*, Vol. III, 451, 452.

consuls, and those in which a State shall be a party. In all other cases, it was provided that the Supreme Court "shall have appellate jurisdiction, both as to law and fact, with such exceptions and under such regulations as the Congress shall make." [47] Answering the objections to the judiciary department, Hamilton asserted in the Federalist the relative weakness of that department. "It" said he, "has no influence over either the sword or the purse; no direction either of the strength or of the wealth of the society; and can take no active resolution whatever. It may truly be said to have neither FORCE nor WILL but merely judgment." He thought it "beyond comparison the weakest of the three departments of power." [48] To some, when the tremendous effect of its power of judgment in deciding upon the validity of legislative acts is considered, the statement appears to be almost ironical. But reflection upon the power of Congress will demonstrate that the Court has found its fortress in public opinion. For, while the Constitution vests the judicial power of the United States in one Supreme Court and in such inferior courts as shall be established by the Congress, and the judicial power cannot be placed elsewhere, still, with respect to the jurisdiction of the Supreme Court, it is only the original jurisdiction that is completely safeguarded by the Constitution. Apart from the cases in which the State is a party, the important jurisdiction is

[47] *Constitution,* Art. III, Sec. 2, par. 2.
[48] *Federalist,* LXXVIII, Vol. 12, p. 256.

appellate and this is subject to "such exceptions" and "such regulations" as the Congress shall make. It is the Congress which constitutes the inferior Federal Courts, and it is Congress which determines what appellate review over these courts the Supreme Court shall have. With Congress responsive to the will of the nation, it is apparent that it is that will which has sustained and has made effective the extraordinary authority of the Supreme Court. The Federal Judiciary Act passed by the Congress in 1789 [49] under the constitutional grant of power has well been called a "transcendent achievement" [50] in the establishment for this country "of the tradition of a system of inferior federal courts." Provision for the appellate jurisdiction of the Supreme Court over State courts was expressly made by Section 25 of that Act in response to the same exigency which led to the creation of the supreme tribunal itself. That exigency still continues and the response from the national legislature remains the same. The judicial organization established by Congress in 1789, due chiefly to the genius of Oliver Ellsworth, a member of the Federal Convention and later Chief Justice of the United States, continued without substantial change for nearly a century. The changes that have been made have been due to the necessity caused by the overwhelming volume of the work of the Court and its arrears of business,

[49] Act of September 24, 1789, 1 *Statutes at Large*, 73.
[50] *Harvard Law Review*, Vol. XXXVIII, 1008; *The Business of the Supreme Court of the United States*, A Study in the Federal Judicial System, Frankfurter and Landis.

which led to the establishment of the Circuit Courts of Appeals as intermediate appellate courts, in 1891. Since then, other limitations of appellate jurisdiction have been made by Congress, with the approval and assistance of the Supreme Court itself, in order to make its exercise of its appellate jurisdiction less a matter of compulsion and thus to enable the Court to have a wide discretion in selecting the cases of a prescribed sort which in its judgment it should review. Determined efforts to cripple the Supreme Court by changing its appellate jurisdiction have not been wanting.[51] In 1868, in the difficult days of reconstruction, the Congress took away from the Court the appellate jurisdiction under the Habeas Corpus Act of 1867, the bill being passed over the President's veto. This was done while an appeal in the celebrated *McCardle* case was actually pending in the Supreme Court, in which it was sought to test the validity of the Reconstruction acts. The Court unanimously decided that the Congress had deprived it of jurisdiction. The Court held that its appellate jurisdiction was derived from the Constitution but was subject to the exceptions made by the Congress, and as the Congress had made a definite exception the Court must abide by it and was not at liberty to inquire into the motives of the legislature.[52]

There have been many violent agitations over the action of the Supreme Court in determining ques-

[51] Warren, *The Supreme Court in United States History,* Vol. II, 22 *et seq.*

[52] *Id.,* Vol. III, 186-210; *Ex parte McCardle,* 7 Wall, 506.

tions of profound public interest. But, despite attacks upon the Court and all proposals to curb it, the Congress from the outset to the present day has actually supported the appellate jurisdiction of the Court in its characteristic features, and the Court thus stands today, not as an organ of government exerting its powers over a reluctant people who find the Constitution difficult of change, but nourished and sustained by the legislative department of the Government responding to public opinion.

It may be doubted if the Supreme Court would have fared so well, if one of the proposals keenly debated in the Federal Convention had been adopted. That was the proposal of James Wilson to have the judiciary united with the Executive in vetoing legislative acts. This was quite distinct from the judicial action contemplated in passing upon the constitutional validity of statutes in the decision of cases before the Court, for it would have associated the judges with the Executive in dealing extrajudicially with questions of policy. Wilson thought that the power of the judges as expositors of the law "did not go far enough." "Laws may be unjust," said he, "may be unwise, may be dangerous, may be destructive and yet may not be so unconstitutional as to justify the Judges in refusing to give them effect. Let them have a share in the Revisionary power, and they will have an opportunity of taking notice of these characters of a law, and of counteracting, by the weight of their opinions the improper views of the Legislature." Ellsworth approved heartily. "The aid of the judges," said he, "will give more wisdom & firmness to the Executive." Madison gave his strong support: "It would be useful to the Judiciary department by giving it an additional opportunity of defending itself against Legislative encroachments; It would be useful to the Executive, by inspiring additional confidence & firmness in exerting the revisionary power: It would be useful to the Legislature by the valuable assistance it would give in preserving a consistency, conciseness, perspicuity & technical propriety in the laws, qualities peculiarly necessary; & yet shamefully wanting in our republican codes. It would moreover be useful to the Community at large as an additional check against a pursuit of those unwise & unjust measures which constituted so great a portion of our calamities." [53] The proposition was debated at length; Wilson, "viewing the subject with all the coolness and attention possible was most apprehensive of a dissolution of the Government from the legislature swallowing up all the other powers." [54]

This practice of associating the judges with a veto power had been adopted in New York in the Constitution of 1777 which provided for a Council of Revision consisting of the Governor, the Chancellor and the judges of the Supreme Court. A majority of this Council could veto any bill which could not become a law except on a two-thirds vote of the legislature overriding the veto. And it may be

[53] *Doc. Hist. Constitution*, Vol. III, 390-392.
[54] *Id.*, Vol. III, 540.

recalled that of 6590 bills passed during the forty years of this practice, only 128 were objected to by the Council.[55] One of the bills which was approved by the Council, with Chancellor Kent as a member, and which he subsequently sustained as a judge, was the statute which the Supreme Court of the United States held to be invalid in *Gibbons* v. *Odgen*,[56] a case which gave the occasion for the classic utterance of Chief Justice Marshall on the supremacy of Congress in its regulation of interstate commerce. Nothing does the Federal Convention greater credit than its capacity, notwithstanding its distrust of legislatures, to resist the plausible arguments of some of its most distinguished members in support of this proposal. It was defeated and the Supreme Court was saved from a union with the Executive which might not have lasted long, but which during the formative period when the court was under attack might well have proved to be destructive of the maintenance of its just authority and influence.

The jurisdiction of the Supreme Court as an independent and exclusively judicial tribunal was thus established. But it was still to prove its adequacy to its task, and its success depended not upon constitutional formulas but on the quality of the men selected and the restraint imposed by the principles which they adopted for the control of their exercise of the judicial power. It may be useful to refer to some of these principles.

[55] Lincoln, *op. cit.*, Vol. I, 744.
[56] 9 Wheaton, 1.

*First.* The Court from the outset has confined itself to its judicial duty of deciding actual cases. This was the intention of the Constitution which expressly provided that the judicial power should extend to "cases" and "controversies." In some States, the authority of their courts to give advisory opinions is expressly granted; not so, in the Federal government. How easy it might have been for the Supreme Court to break over this limitation or to obscure it by a broad construction is shown by the fact that at the very beginning its opinion was sought by President Washington, on the advice of his Cabinet, with respect to a series of questions in relation to the Genet controversy. The question related to the interpretation of our treaties with France. The court replied to President Washington that it considered it improper to declare opinions on questions not growing out of a case before it.[57]

There was an extraordinary incident in President Monroe's administration. The President sent his long argument on internal improvements to the Justices of the Supreme Court. Justice Johnson wrote to the President that he had been "instructed to make the following Report. The Judges are deeply sensible of the mark of Confidence bestowed on them in this Instance and should be unworthy of that Confidence did they attempt to conceal their real Opinion. Indeed to conceal or disavow it would be now impossible as they are all of Opinion that the Deci-

[57] Warren, *op. cit.*, Vol. I, 108-111.

sion on the Bank question [58] completely commits them on the Subject of internal Improvement as applied to Post-roads and Military Roads. On the other Points it is impossible to resist the lucid and conclusive Reasoning contained in the argument." [59] This, of course, was extra-official, but it is safe to say that nothing of the sort could happen today. The Court has rejected the overtures of the Congress for opinions on constitutional questions in the absence of a real "case" or "controversy" to be decided. It was not long ago (1911) (*Muskrat* v. *United States*)[60] that the Supreme Court decided that Congress had no power to pass an act conferring jurisdiction on the Court of Claims, and, on appeal, upon the Supreme Court, to determine the validity of acts of Congress relating to Indian matters without "a case" or "controversy" to which alone, under the Constitution, the judicial power extends. This principle of action is of general application in the work of the Federal courts. Within a few weeks, the Supreme Court has held that the Federal District court had no jurisdiction of a suit instituted in Kentucky by a trading concern to obtain a judgment declaring their rights under an act of the Kentucky legislature (1924) regulating sales of leaf tobacco. The sole purpose of the suit was to obtain a declaration of the rights and duties of the plaintiffs under

[58] *McCulloch v. Maryland,* 4 Wheaton, 316.

[59] Monroe MSS. (Library of Cong.), Vol. 20, fol. 2568; Warren, *op. cit.,* Vol. II, 56.

[60] 219 U. S. 346.

this statute and the extent to which they must comply with it in the course of their business. The Commonwealth attorney was made defendant but the Court found that there was no semblance of any adverse litigation with him individually nor any charge that he had threatened or contemplated any action against the plaintiff for violation of law either actual or prospective.[61] The determination of constitutional questions has been associated with the strictly judicial function and so far as possible has been removed from the contentions of politics. These questions have been decided after full argument in contested cases and it is only with the light afforded by a real contest that opinions on questions of the highest importance can safely be rendered.

The Supreme Court has also determined that neither legislative nor administrative jurisdiction can be conferred upon it either directly or by appeal. The Act of Congress of March 23, 1792,[62] required the Circuit Courts of the United States to examine into the claims of the officers and soldiers and seamen of the Revolution to the pensions granted to invalids by that Act, to determine the amount of pay that would be equivalent to the disability incurred, and to certify their opinion to the Secretary of War. The judges in the New York Circuit, composed of Chief Justice Jay, Justice Cushing and Duane, District Judge, held that the power could not be exercised by them as a court, but, in consideration of the

---

[61] *Liberty-Warehouse Co. v. Grannis,* 273 U. S. 70.
[62] 1 *Statutes at Large,* 243.

meritorious and benevolent object of the law, they agreed to construe the power as conferred on them individually as commissioners. The judges of the Pennsylvania Circuit, consisting of Wilson and Blair, Justices of the Supreme Court, and Peters, District Judge, refused to execute it altogether, upon the ground that the authority was conferred on them as a court, and was not a judicial power. Other judges held the matter under advisement. Later the case came before the Supreme Court of the United States and it was decided that the power given in the Act of 1792 to the Circuit Courts could not be construed to give it to the judges out of court as commissioners and that their action as such was invalid.[63] The principle involved was recently stated and applied by Chief Justice Taft in delivering the opinion of the Court in the case of *Keller* v. *Potomac Electric Power Company.*[64] It was there decided that Congress cannot confer power upon the Supreme Court to review, on appeal from another reviewing court (in that case, the Court of Appeals of the District of Columbia), the legislative discretion of a public utilities commission in fixing rates for public service corporation so as to enable the court to consider the facts and fix the rate which the commission should have made.

*Second.* A second principle is that the Court will not deal with questions which are regarded as pure-

[63] See *United States v. Todd*, 13 Howard, 52, *note.*
[64] 261 U. S. 428.

ly political in their nature rather than judicial. A controversy of this sort grew out of the Dorr Revolution in Rhode Island in 1841. The constitution of that State had provided for a very limited suffrage which caused intense dissatisfaction. Failing in efforts to amend the constitution, mass meetings were held and associations were formed which re-sulted in the election, without the authorization of the existing government, of delegates to what has been called a "voluntary convention." This body framed a constitution, provided for its ratification by the people and under this constitution a new gov-ernment was set up which was not recognized by the old or so-called charter government. One of the representatives of the old government broke into the house of one Martin Luther, who was active in the support of the new government of which Thomas W. Dorr was the head, and Luther brought action for trespass. The controversy reached the Supreme Court. Party feeling was exceedingly bitter as Dorr represented a popular cause and had wide political support throughout the country. Webster, the expounder of the Constitution, represented the charter government and argued that "our American mode of government does not derive any power from tumultuous assemblies." He insisted that "when it is necessary to ascertain the will of the people, the legislature must provide the means of ascertaining it." And he invoked the provision of Section 4 of Article IV of the Federal Constitution that "the United States shall guarantee to every State in this

Union a Republican Form of Government and shall
protect each of them against Invasion." Nathan
Clifford, then Attorney General in President Polk's
cabinet and later a Justice of the Supreme Court of
the United States, answered Mr. Webster. The
arguments of both received the highest praise. The
Court regarded the question as purely political and
declined to decide it. Chief Justice Taney delivered
the opinion which held, with only one Justice dissenting, that under the article granting a republican
form of government it rests with the Congress to
decide what government is the established one in a
State and whether it is republican or not; and that
when Senators and Representatives of a State are
admitted into the councils of the Union the authority
of the Government under which they are appointed,
as well as its republican character, is recognized by
the proper constitutional authority. The decision
of that authority was held to be binding upon every
other department of the Government and not to be
open to question in a judicial tribunal. "If the judicial power extends so far," said Chief Justice
Taney, "the guarantee contained in the Constitution
of the United States is a guarantee of anarchy, and
not of order." [65] On similar ground suits brought by
Mississippi and Georgia to restrain the execution of
the Reconstruction Acts passed after the Civil War
were dismissed.

A few years ago there was another effort to obtain
from the Supreme Court a decision, as to the appli-

[65] *Luther v. Borden,* 7 Howard, 1, 43.

cation of the guaranty to the States of a republican form of government, in a case from Oregon involving the validity of the amendment to the Constitution of that State providing for the enactment of laws through the initiative and referendum. The Court declined to consider the question. In the opinion of the Court, Chief Justice White observed: "The suggestion but results from failing to distinguish between things which are widely different, that is, the legislative duty to determine the political questions involved in deciding whether a state government republican in form exists, and the judicial power and ever-present duty whenever it becomes necessary in a controversy properly submitted to enforce and uphold the applicable provisions of the Constitution as to each and every exercise of governmental power." [66]

*Third.*  The Court will not undertake to decide questions of the constitutional validity of legislation unless these questions are necessarily presented and must be determined. The Court considers it to be its duty in construing a statute which is reasonably susceptible of two constructions, one of which would make it unconstitutional and the other valid, to adopt that construction which saves its constitutionality. As a corollary, the Court will construe a statute, if it admits of two constructions, so as to avoid if possible the decision of a doubtful constitutional ques-

[66] *Pacific States Telephone & Telegraph Co., v. Oregon*, 223 U. S. 118, 150.

tion. This is a self-denying rule which may sometimes have the effect of putting a strain upon the interpretation of a Congressional enactment in order to uphold it. A striking illustration is the limited construction given to the commodities clause of the Hepburn Act of 1906, because it was found that if the Court gave to the clause the broad effect, for which the Government contended, grave constitutional questions would be presented. Thus a statute held wholly void by the court below was strictly construed and sustained.[67]

*Fourth.* Another established principle is that the Supreme Court does not undertake to review questions of legislative policy. Here we meet one of the pleasant assumptions which make our system of government workable. For the purposes of the courts, the legislature within its sphere is deemed to possess all available knowledge and to be the treasure house of wisdom. So long as it acts within the limits of legislative power, the actualities of legislative processes are not the subject of judicial consideration.

When the Court is dealing with the question whether a legislative act is arbitrary, and transcends the limits of reason which are deemed to be embraced in the fundamental conception of due process of law or of equal protection of the laws, it may be difficult to draw the line between what is regarded as wholly unreasonable and what is deemed to be unwise. It

[67] *United States v. Delaware & Hudson Co.*, 213 U. S. 366.

is doubtless true that men holding strong convictions as to the unwisdom of legislation may easily pass to the position that it is wholly unreasonable. But the distinction nevertheless exists and it is ever present to the conscientious judge. He recognizes that there is a wide domain of legislative discretion before constitutional boundaries are reached, and he holds himself to the duty of not allowing his views of the proper exercise of that discretion to control. He does his work in an objective spirit. If it be said that this is an impossible degree of self-control and that, even with the most conscientious judge, political and economic views will sway the judgment, albeit unconsciously, it may be answered that judges are constantly sustaining the validity of legislation which as legislators they would probably condemn. I think it may be said that judges who have gained a distinct reputation for their liberal attitude, in sustaining in close cases the legislative power with respect to measures which have engaged popular attention and have been directed to the achievement of social purposes through interference with individual freedom of action, have often entertained profound distrust of the policy of the legislative acts they were holding to be within the authority of the Congress or of the State legislatures. The distinction between questions of mere wisdom or policy and those of power has been applied in a multitude of cases. In dealing with the child labor cases, from the standpoint of the power of the Congress, the Court manifestly was not considering child labor from an economic or humanitarian point of view. Every member of the Court might be opposed to child labor although unable to sustain the particular act as being within the power of Congress. So, in questions arising under the Eighteenth Amendment and the Volstead Act, the judges are not deciding cases as "wets" or "drys" but are interpreting the statute and the Constitution quite apart from their personal or political views as to the policy of prohibition.

The corollary of this principle is that the Court will not inquire into the motives of Congress or of the State legislature. As was said by Mr. Justice Brandeis in delivering the opinion of the Supreme Court sustaining the wartime prohibition act: "No principle of our constitutional law is more firmly established than that this court may not, in passing upon the validity of a statute, enquire into the motives of Congress." [68]

The Court has gone very far in this view in sustaining the exercise of the Federal taxing power. But it is obvious that it might go so far that Congress under the guise of the taxing power could destroy all the reserved rights of the States. As Chief Justice Taft said in the recent child labor case with respect to the presumption of validity appearing on the face of the statute: "Grant the validity of this law, and all that Congress would need to do, hereafter, in seeking to take over to its control

[68] *Hamilton v. Kentucky Distilleries & Warehouse Co.*, 251 U. S 146, 161.

any one of the great number of subjects of public interest, jurisdiction of which the States have never parted with, and which are reserved to them by the Tenth Amendment, would be to enact a detailed measure of complete regulation of the subject and enforce it by a so-called tax upon departures from it. To give such magic to the word 'tax' would be to break down all constitutional limitation of the powers of Congress and completely wipe out the sovereignty of the States.'' The Chief Justice then drew the distinction between a tax and a penalty and while pointing out that taxes are occasionally imposed in the discretion of the legislature on proper subjects with the primary motive of obtaining revenue from them and with the incidental motive of discouraging them by making their continuance onerous, such taxes do not lose their character as taxes because of the incidental motive. ''But there comes a time,'' said he, ''in the extension of the penalizing features of the so-called tax when it loses its character as such and becomes a mere penalty with the characteristics of regulation and punishment.''[69] Such was the case then before the Court. When the imposition is found to be a penalty, the Court must ascertain the authority of Congress to impose it as a feature, not of a tax law, but of a regulation of the subject with respect to which the penalty is imposed.

I have referred to these principles to show that the success of the work of the Supreme Court in

[69] *Bailey v. Drexel Furniture Co.*, 259 U. S. 20, 38; see also, *Trusler v. Crooks*, 269 U. S. 475.

maintaining the necessary balance between State and Nation, and between individual rights as guaranteed by the Constitution and social interest as expressed in legislation, has been due largely to the deliberate determination of the Court to confine itself to its judicial task, and, while careful to maintain its authority as the interpreter of the Constitution, the Court has not sought to aggrandize itself at the expense of either executive or legislature.

# II

## The Court at Work — Organization — Methods

Under the Judiciary Act of 1789,[1] provision was made for a Supreme Court consisting of a Chief Justice and five Associate Justices. The number of Associate Justices was increased to six in the year 1807, to eight in 1837 and to nine in 1863. An act of 1866[2] would in time have reduced the Associate Justices to six, but unfilled vacancies had cut the number to seven when the Act of 1869[3] reconstituted the Court with a Chief Justice and eight Associate Justices, or nine in all, as it remains at the present time.

Ten Chief Justices and sixty-five Associate Justices have served in the Court, including those now on the bench. Washington made four appointments to the office of Chief Justice; John Jay, who served from 1789 to 1795 and then resigned to accept appointment as special Ambassador to England; John Rutledge who was appointed in 1795 during a recess of the Senate and was rejected when his name was sent in; William Cushing who was appointed, confirmed and declined; Oliver Ellsworth who served from 1796 to 1800 and resigned to become Ambass-

[1] 1 *Statutes at Large*, 73.
[2] 14 *id.*, 209.
[3] 16 *id.*, 44.

ador to France. President Adams then appointed
John Jay as Chief Justice who declined, and John
Marshall was appointed in 1801. From that time
until 1864 there were only two Chief Justices, —
Marshall who served until 1835 and his successor,
Roger B. Taney, who remained on the bench until
1864. Then followed, as Chief Justices, Salmon P.
Chase, for eight years, Morrison R. Waite for fifteen
years, Melville W. Fuller for twenty-two years, Ed-
ward D. White for ten years and the present Chief
Justice, William H. Taft.

Washington appointed no less than nine to the
office of Associate Justice. Rutledge resigned before sitting with the Court as he preferred to be
Chief Justice of South Carolina. Robert H. Harrison declined in order to become Chancellor of Maryland. The others appointed by Washington were
Wilson, Cushing, Blair, Iredell, Johnson, Paterson
and Samuel Chase. Of these, Wilson, Blair, Iredell,
and Cushing either had been members of the Federal
Convention or were strong supporters of the ratification of the Constitution.

Three Presidents, since Washington, have appoint-
ed a controlling number of the members of the
Court, — Jackson, Lincoln and Taft. President
Jackson appointed Chief Justice Taney and four
Associate Justices, all being Democrats. President
Lincoln appointed Chief Justice Chase and four As-
sociate Justices (including Samuel F. Miller and
Stephen J. Field), two Republicans, two Independ-
ents and one Democrat. President Taft appointed

Chief Justice White and five Associate Justices, three Republicans and three Democrats. Two appointments for Chief Justice were withdrawn after their names had been sent to the Senate, — George H. Williams of Oregon and Caleb Cushing of Massachusetts, both nominated by President Grant. Several, nominated as Associate Justices, have been rejected by the Senate, including such distinguished lawyers as Jeremiah S. Black, Ebenezer Rockwell Hoar, William B. Hornblower and Wheeler H. Peckham. Many appointees have declined, among others, John Quincy Adams and Roscoe Conkling, both of whom declined after being confirmed.

It is manifest that geographical considerations should not control at the expense of exceptional fitness in determining appointments to the Supreme Court. Yet the confidence of the country should be maintained by selections which so far as practicable will represent all parts of the United States. It is interesting to note that appointments have been made from twenty-six States and while twenty-two States have been unrepresented there has been little ground for complaint as appointments have been made from other States in the same general area. New York has had the largest number of appointments, that is, nine; Massachusetts and Ohio come next with seven; then Pennsylvania, Tennessee and Virginia with five. Taking the nine circuits as at present constituted, appointments have been made as follows: From the first, nine; the second, eleven; the third, eight; the fourth, thirteen; the fifth, seven;

the sixth, sixteen; the seventh, two; the eighth, five; the ninth, two. No appointments in the fourth circuit consisting of Maryland, Virginia and West Virginia, and the Carolinas, have been made since the Civil War, but it should be remembered that Chief Justice White of Louisiana and Associate Justice Lurton of Tennessee, both appointed by a Republican President, had served in the Confederate Army.

Justices of the Supreme Court are appointed and confirmed by the political departments of the Government. But an examination of the work of the Supreme Court discloses a most gratifying freedom from control by political parties. It has been shown abundantly that, while fundamental political principles have been held strongly, the judges have not been subject to influence by party machinery or by either visible or invisible government. Judges as men of mature years and wide experience undoubtedly have their convictions, political and economic, their views of the nature and purpose of our Government, of the relation of the judicial department to the working of the Government, but they have not been the instruments of political manipulations or the tools of power. One cannot study their lives and decisions without confidence in their sincerity and independence. The Supreme Court has the inevitable failings of any human institution, but it has vindicated the confidence, which underlies the success of democratic effort, that you can find in imperfect human beings, for the essential administration of justice, a rectitude of purpose, a clarity of vision and a capacity for independence, impartiality and balanced judgment which will render impotent the solicitation of friends, the appeals of erstwhile political associates, and the threats of enemies.

The Supreme Court has had at all times the most severe critics. Marshall and his associates buttressed the foundations of a strong national government. Jefferson exclaimed that "the judiciary of the United States is the subtle corps of sappers and miners constantly working under ground to undermine the foundations of our Confederated fabric. They are construing our Constitution from a co-ordination of a general and special government to a general and supreme one alone. This will lay all things at their feet, and they are too well versed in English law to forget the maxim, *'boni judicis est ampliare jurisdictionem'*." [4] In a later period when other doctrines seemed to be paramount Kent, in writing to Justice Story, said: "I have lost my confidence and hopes in the constitutional guardianship and protection of the Supreme Court." [5] And again he could say: "What a succession of great & estimable men have you witnessed as Associates since you ascended the Bench, and now what a 'melancholy mass' it presents!" [6] But great critics are even more apt to display their infirmities than great judges acting under a keener sense of responsibility. Good and

[4] Letter to Thomas Ritchie, Dec. 25, 1820, Jefferson's *Works*, Vol. 7, p. 191.

[5] Story, *Life and Letters of Joseph Story*, Vol. II, p. 270.

[6] Letter of June 17, 1845; Mass. Hist. Soc. *Proc.*, 2d Ser. XIV, p. 420; Warren, *op. cit.* Vol. II. p. 415.

able men have always dealt unsparingly with the conduct of equally good and able men who cherish different opinions; and perhaps the judicial branch of the Government has suffered much less in such estimates than either the executive or legislative. Mr. Warren has given us the following striking summary: "Judges appointed by Jefferson and Madison did not hesitate to join with Marshall in sustaining and developing the strongly Nationalistic interpretation of the Constitution so obnoxious to Jefferson. Judges appointed by Jackson joined with Marshall and Story in supporting the Cherokee Missionaries against Georgia, in flat opposition to Jackson. The whole Bench appointed by Jackson decided against his policy in relation to the Spanish land claims. Judges appointed by Jackson and Van Buren threw down the gauntlet to the former by issuing a mandamus against his favorite Postmaster-General. In every case involving slavery, anti-slavery Judges joined with pro-slavery Judges in rendering the decisions. The constitutionality of the obnoxious Fugitive Slave Law was unanimously upheld by anti-slavery Whig Judges and by pro-slavery Democrats alike. A Northern Democrat joined with a Northern Whig Judge in dissenting in the *Dred Scott Case*. President Lincoln's Legal Tender policy was held unconstitutional by his own appointees. The Reconstruction policies and acts of the Republican Party were held unconstitutional by a Republican Bench. The constitutional views of the Democratic Party as to our insular possessions were opposed by a Democratic Judge who joined with his Republican Associates in making up the majority in the *Insular Cases.*" He adds that "nothing is more striking in the history of the Court than the manner in which the hopes of those who expected a Judge to follow the political views of the President appointing him have been disappointed." [7]

An outstanding instance of the change in view which may come with the conscious responsibility of judicial office is shown by the opinion of Chief Justice Chase in the first legal tender case holding the act to be unconstitutional which as Secretary of the Treasury he had favored. He explained: "It is not surprising that amid the tumult of the late civil war, and under the influence of apprehensions for the safety of the Republic almost universal, different views, never before entertained by American statesmen or jurists, were adopted by many. The time was not favorable to considerate reflection upon the constitutional limits of legislative or executive authority." [8] I may give two other illustrations. President Roosevelt was deeply interested in the prosecution and success of the suit brought to dissolve the Northern Securities Company. He had appointed two Associate Justices, but one of these, Justice Holmes,[9] joined with the appointees of President Cleveland in dissent, writing a strong opinion

[7] Warren, *op. cit.*, Vol. I, pp. 21, 22.

[8] *Hepburn v. Griswold*, 8 Wallace, 603, 625.

[9] See *Correspondence of Theodore Roosevelt and Henry Cabot Lodge*, Vol. I, p. 517.

against the contentions of the Government.[10]   Very
recently the Supreme Court decided a question which
had remained open from the foundation of the Government as to the President's power of removal.
The case arose out of the action of President Wilson
in removing a Postmaster of the first class without
the advice and consent of the Senate, although the
Postmaster had been appointed under an act of Congress which provided for removal with such advice
and consent.   President Wilson's action was sustained by the Court in an opinion delivered by the
Chief Justice, a former Republican President, but
both the Associate Justices appointed by President
Wilson, Justice McReynolds, who had been Attorney
General under President Wilson, and Justice Brandeis dissented, being of the opinion that the action
of the President had been outside his constitutional
power. [11]   If conscientious, able and independent men
are put on the bench, you cannot predict their course
as judges by reference either to partisan motives or
to personal or party loyalties.   If you could get further down to the bedrock of conviction as to what are
conceived to be fundamental principles of government and social relations, you might be able to get
closer to accurate prophecy.   But you cannot expect
to have judges worthy of the office who are without
convictions and the question from that point of view
is not as to the qualifications of judges but whether
you will have a court of this character and function.

[10] *Northern Securities Co. v. United States,* 193 U. S. 197, 400.
[11] *Myers v. United States,* 272 U. S. 52.

Putting aside the long course of criticism of the Court, bitter and unrelenting, neither the occasion nor the grounds of which I can take time to review, with respect to which the Court has either been vindicated in public opinion or the criticism has had but slight effect upon the general reputation of the Court, it remains true that in three notable instances the Court has suffered severely from self-inflicted wounds. The first of these was the *Dred Scott* case.[12] Von Holst said that it had been the systematic and conscious aim of the South to make the Supreme Court the citadel of slaveocracy and that the *Dred Scott* decision was a witness of the success of their efforts. There the Supreme Court decided that Dred Scott, a negro, not being a citizen could not sue in the United States Courts and that Congress could not prohibit slavery in the territories. Assuming the sincerity of the judges who took this view, the grave injury that the Court sustained through its decision has been universally recognized. Its action was a public calamity. The decision was greeted by the anti-slavery papers in the North with derision and contempt. There were not lacking more conservative expressions and there was support from strong Democratic papers, but the widespread and bitter attacks upon the judges who joined in the decision undermined confidence in the Court. False and scurrilous comments upon the traits and character of the judges supplemented hostile analysis of Chief Justice Taney's opinion. Lincoln riddled

[12] *Scott v. Sandford,* 19 Howard, 393.

the decision in his speeches, but he gave due respect to the judicial institution. He said in the course of his debate with Douglas: "We believe as much as Judge Douglas (perhaps more) in obedience to and respect for the judicial department of government. We think its decisions on constitutional questions, when fully settled, should control, not only the particular cases decided, but the general policy of the country, subject to be disturbed only by amendments of the Constitution as provided in that instrument itself. More than this would be revolution . But we think the *Dred Scott* decision is erroneous. We know the court that made it has often overruled its own decisions, and we shall do what we can to have it overrule this. We offer no resistance to it." [13] It was many years before the Court, even under new judges , was able to retrieve its reputation.

It was during this period, while the Court was still suffering from lack of a satisfactory measure of public confidence, that another decision was rendered which brought the Court into disesteem. I refer to the legal tender cases decided in 1870. It has repeatedly been sought to use for political purposes the power of Congress to fix the number of justices. In 1866, Congress had provided for a reduction in the number in order to deprive President Johnson of the opportunity to make appointments and, after that danger was passed and Grant had become Pres-

[13] June 26, 1857; *Abraham Lincoln, Complete Works*, Nicolay and Hay, Vol. I, 228.

ident, the number of the justices was increased to
nine. While there were two vacancies on the Court,
the case of *Hepburn* v. *Griswold* [14] involving the
validity of the legal tender act passed during the
Civil War was decided, the Court holding the act to
be unconstitutional as to contracts made before its
passage and indicating in the reasoning of its opinion that the act was also invalid as to contracts
subsequently made. The decision was by a bench of
seven, and three Justices dissented. On the day that
the opinion was delivered by Chief Justice Chase,
President Grant nominated William Strong of Pennsylvania and Joseph P. Bradley of New Jersey to
fill the two vacancies. The action of the Court,
taken soon after their confirmation, in ordering a reargument of the constitutional question and then
deciding that the legal tender act was constitutional,[15] the two new judges joining with the three
judges, who had dissented in the *Hepburn* case, to
make a majority, caused widespread criticism.
From the standpoint of the effect on public opinion,
there can be no doubt that the reopening of the case
was a serious mistake and the overruling in such a
short time, and by one vote, of the previous decision
shook popular respect for the Court. There was no
ground for attacking the honesty of the judges or
for the suggestion that President Grant had attempted to pack the Court. Both the new judges were
able and honest men, Justice Bradley being one of

[14] 8 Wallace, 603.
[15] *Knox v. Lee,* 12 Wallace, 457.

the strongest men who have sat on the bench. President Grant stated that he knew nothing of the decision of the Court at the time of the appointment,
and it has well been said that in view of the fact that
every prominent Republican lawyer apparently considered the legal tender act to be constitutional and
practically every State Court had so held it would
have been difficult for the President to find any
qualified men of his own party who had any other
opinion. The Court alone was responsible for the
unfortunate effect of its change of front and for its
action in reopening the case which might well have
been considered closed. The argument for reopening was strongly presented in view of the great importance of the question, but the effect of such a sud-
den reversal of judgment might easily have been
foreseen. Stability in judicial opinions is of no little importance in maintaining respect for the Court's
work.

Twenty-five years later, when the Court had re-
covered its prestige, its action in the income tax
cases gave occasion for a bitter assault. Here again,
there was not the slightest ground for criticism of
of the integrity of the judges who participated in
the decision. Nor did the actual decision against
the validity of the tax furnish basis for anything
more than the conflict, even of expert opinion, which
attaches to the determination of difficult constitutional questions. The circumstance which caught
the public imagination and which ever since has
furnished occasion for disparaging comment, was

that after the question of the validity of the income
tax with respect to income from personal property
as such, and the question whether the provision held
void with respect to income from real estate as a
direct and unapportioned tax invalidated the whole
act, had been reserved owing to an equal division of
the Court,[16] a reargument was ordered and in the
second decision the act was held to be unconstitutional by a majority of one.[17]  Justice Jackson
was ill at the time of the first argument but
took part in the final decision, voting in favor of
the validity of the statute.[18]  It was evident that the
result was brought about by a change in the vote of
one of the judges who had participated in the first
decision.  There can be no objection to a conscientious judge changing his vote, but the decision of
such an important question by a majority of one
after one judge had changed his vote aroused a criticism of the Court which has never been entirely
stilled.  At the time, the most bitter attacks were
made upon Justice Shiras, who was popularly
supposed to have been the one who changed his vote.
He bore the criticism with a calm dignity, but there
is good reason to believe that the charge was without
foundation and that he was not the member of the
Court whose views were altered on the reargument.
The demand for a Federal income tax culminated in
the adoption of the Sixteenth Amendment authoriz-
ing a federal income tax without apportionment.

[16] *Pollock v. Farmers' Loan & Trust Co.*, 157 U. S. 429, 586.
[17] *Id.*, 158 U. S. 601.
[18] *Id.*, 158 U. S. 696.

When, however, we consider the hundred and thirty-six years of the Court's activities, the thousands of its determinations, the difficult questions with which it has dealt, and the fact that it has come out of its conflicts with its wounds healed, with its integrity universally recognized, with its ability giving it a rank second to none among the judicial tribunals of the world, and that today no institution of our government stands higher in public confidence, we must realize that this is due, whatever may be thought as to the necessity of the function it performs, to the impartial manner in which the Court addresses itself to its never-ending task, to the unsullied honor, the freedom from political entanglements and the expertness of the judges who are bearing the heaviest burden of severe and continuous intellectual work that our country knows.

How is this work performed? What is its method?

A word may be said as to the volume of work. At the time of Marshall's appointment (1801) the Chief Justiceship was said to be a sinecure. In that year, only ten cases were brought before the Court. The entire number during the next five years was 120. Thereafter the business of the Court increased until between 1826 and 1830 the number of cases rose to an annual average of 58. From that time until 1850 the increase was gradual, until the average was 71 a year. At the beginning of the term in 1860 the number of cases on the docket was 278. In the next twenty-five years there was an enormous increase due to the questions growing out of the Civil War, reconstruction, amendments to the Constitution and the establishment of the Court of Claims. Thus, in 1880, at the close of the second week of the term, the number of cases set for argument reached 1069; in 1889, 1478.[19] The establishment of the Circuit Courts of Appeals under the act of 1891 greatly relieved the Supreme Court and subsequent restrictions of its appellate jurisdiction have enabled the Court to keep fairly abreast of its work. The number on the docket at the beginning of the current term (October Term, 1926) was 667, of which 438 cases were brought forward from the preceding term. A case which is not advanced out of its order, as many cases are, can now be reached for argument in from twelve to fifteen months after it has been docketed.

Popular interest naturally centers in the Chief Justice as the titular head of the Court. He is its executive officer; he presides at its sessions and at its conferences, and announces its orders. By virtue of the distinctive function of the Court he is the most important judicial officer in the world; he is the Chief Justice of the United States. In relation to the actual determinations of the Court, however, he is one of nine judges having no greater authority than any of his brethren in the decision of cases. It should also be observed that in the Supreme Court, aside from administrative matters of the merest routine, every action of the Court is taken on the con-

[19] *North American Review*, May, 1881, Vol. 132, p. 437; November, 1890, Vol. 151, p. 568.

currence of a majority of its members. Every Justice has the opportunity to vote upon every question. It is the practice of the Court that such a vote shall be taken and the opinion of the majority ascertained before a case is referred to one of the Justices for the writing of an opinion. In this way the entire Court participates in its judicial work.

The Chief Justice as the head of the Court has an outstanding position, but in a small body of able men with equal authority in the making of decisions, it is evident that his actual influence will depend upon the strength of his character and the demonstration of his ability in the intimate relations of the judges. It is safe to say that no member of the Supreme Court is under any illusion as to the mental equipment of his brethren. Constant and close association discloses the strength and exposes the weaknesses of each. Courage of conviction, sound learning, familiarity with precedents, exact knowledge due to painstaking study of the cases under consideration cannot fail to command that profound respect which is always yielded to intellectual power conscientiously applied. That influence can be exerted by any member of the Court, whatever his rank in the order of precedence. At the conference of the Supreme Court, where after arguments have been heard and records and briefs have been examined, the members of the Court compare their views and register their decisions, not only the cases under review but the mental equipment and character of the judges are necessarily subject to the closest observation. Marshall's preeminence was due to the fact that he was John Marshall, not simply that he was Chief Justice; the combination of John Marshall and the Chief Justiceship has given us our most illustrious judicial figure. But there have been great leaders on the bench who were not Chief Justices. Such a man was Joseph Story. Benjamin R. Curtis stands out conspicuously in the time of Taney. Salmon P. Chase, Morrison R. Waite and Melville W. Fuller were jurists of high distinction and discharged with conspicuous ability the duties of their office, as Chief Justice, but they gained nothing by virtue of their headship of the Court over such men as Samuel F. Miller, Stephen J. Field, Joseph P. Bradley, Horace Gray, and David J. Brewer, who as Associate Justices rose to a level of achievement in their judicial work second only to that of Marshall. Edward D. White in the quality of his work was as distinguished while Associate Justice as in his Chief Justiceship.

While the Chief Justice has only one vote, the way in which the Court does its work gives him a special opportunity for leadership. At the conference it is the practice for the Chief Justice, unless he desires otherwise, to be the first to state his opinion with respect to the case to be decided; he gives his opinion first and votes last. After a decision has been reached, the Chief Justice assigns the case for opinion to one of the members of the Court, that is, of course, to one of the majority if there is a division and the Chief Justice is a member of the majority.

If he is in a minority, the senior Associate Justice in the majority assigns the case for opinion. When assigning cases, the Chief Justice may retain any cases he pleases for himself. It is recognized that he has sole control over the assignment of opinions and his assignments are never questioned. In this way he has an important choice among the judges in the distribution of important cases. It would naturally be the effort of the Chief Justice to distribute the work so that each judge would have about the same amount of work as the others and about the same proportion of important cases. It might be supposed that this method would be open to objection, but it has worked well. I regard it as far better than the method of some Courts of assigning cases in rotation so that the judges know when the case is argued, unless there is some division making a different assignment necessary, who is going to write the opinion. In the Supreme Court every judge comes to the conference to express his views and to vote, not knowing but that he may have the responsibility of writing the opinion which will accord with the vote. He is thus keenly aware of his responsibility in voting. It is not the practice in the Supreme Court to postpone voting until an opinion has been brought in by one of the judges which may be plausible enough to win the adherence of another judge who has not studied the case carefully. In referring to this, I am not revealing confidences which I gained during my term of office. The practice of the Court was then, and I believe that it still remains, the same as it was described by John A. Campbell in his eulogy, in 1874, of Benjamin R. Curtis. Both Campbell and Curtis had sat on the bench with Chief Justice Taney and both had resigned. Campbell thus described the methods of the Court: "The duties of the Justices of the Supreme Court consist in the hearing of cases; the preparations for the consultations; the consultations in the conference of the judges; the decision of the cause there, and the preparation of the opinion and the judgment of the court. Their most arduous and responsible duty is in the conference. * * * In these conferences, the Chief Justice usually called the case. He stated the pleadings and facts that they presented, the arguments and his conclusions in regard to them, and invited discussion. The discussion was free and open among the Justices till all were satisfied. The question was put, whether the judgment or decree should be reversed, and each Justice, according to his precedence, commencing with the junior judge, was required to give his judgment and his reasons for his conclusion. The concurring opinions of the majority decided the cause and signified the matter of the opinion to be given. The Chief Justice designated the judge to prepare it." [20]

Story tells us of the methods of his day (1812) and the long arguments to which the Court listened: "The mode of arguing causes in the Supreme Court is excessively prolix and tedious; but generally the subject is exhausted, and it is not very difficult to

[20] 20 Wallace, *Mem.,* X.

perceive at the close of the cause, in many cases, where the press of the argument and of the law lies. We moot every question as we proceed, and my familiar conferences at our lodgings often come to a very quick, and, I trust, a very accurate opinion, in a few hours. * * * Many of our causes are of extreme intricacy. * * * One great cause of the Holland Land Company, of which I had a printed brief of two hundred and thirty pages, lasted five days in argument, and has now been happily decided.''[21]

In the early period when cases were few, the Court could permit extended argument. At a more recent time, and until a few years ago, two hours was the regular allowance to each side and in very important cases that time was extended. This allowance has been reduced to an hour, unless special permission is granted, and even in cases of great importance the Court has refused to hear arguments for more than an hour and a half on each side. This restriction is due to the crowded calendar of the Court. The progress of civilization is but little reflected in the processes of argumentation and a vast amount of time is unavoidably wasted in the Supreme Court in listening to futile discussion; this has the effect of reducing the time for cases which should be fully presented. I suppose that, aside from cases of exceptional difficulty, the impression that a judge has at the close of a full oral argument accords with the conviction which controls his final vote. A Judge

[21] Story, *Life and Letters of Joseph Story,* Vol. I, p. 215; Warren, *op. cit.,* Vol. I, pp. 423, 424.

of the Court of Appeals of New York told me some years ago that he had kept track for a time of his impressions after the oral arguments and found that in ninety per centum of the cases, although, of course, he reserved his vote until after a thorough study, his final judgment agreed with his view at the end of the oral argument. This is so because the judges are conversant with their special material, that is, the prior decisions of the court, and when they apprehend the precise question to be decided they are generally not slow in reaching a conclusion. The judges of the Supreme Court are quite free in addressing questions to counsel during argument. The Bar is divided as to the wisdom of this practice in courts of last resort. Some think that as a rule the court will get at the case more quickly if counsel are permitted to present it in their own way. Well-prepared and experienced counsel, however, do not object to inquiries from the bench, if the time allowed for argument is not unduly curtailed, as they would much prefer to have the opportunity of knowing the difficulties in the minds of the court and of attempting to meet them rather than to have them concealed and presented in conference when counsel are not present. They prefer an open attack to a masked battery. From the standpoint of the bench, the desirability of questions is quite obvious as the judges are not there to listen to speeches but to decide the case. They have an irrepressible desire for immediate knowledge as to the points to be determined. The desirability, however, of a full exposition by oral argument in the highest court is not to be gainsaid. It is a great saving of time of the court, in the examination of extended records and briefs, to obtain the grasp of the case that is made possible by oral discussion and to be able more quickly to separate the wheat from the chaff. Our records in these days of typing are apt to be full of chaff. The oral argument is supplemented by briefs which present in an extended manner the various points and the authorities in support of them. If oral arguments are compressed by a time allowance, briefs are not, and the judges have to contend with their diffuseness. But if a brief is well arranged and properly indexed, the judges can readily find the points they wish to examine. Whatever the character of the arguments, oral and written, the judge must understand the record and the points when he comes to conference. In Campbell's tribute to Curtis, from which I have quoted, he referred to the eminent service rendered by Curtis in the conference because of his careful preparation and his exact knowledge. Judge Campbell said as to this: "It was here that the merits of Justice Curtis were most conspicuous to his associates. * * * Justice Curtis always came to the conference with full cognizance of the case, the pleadings, facts, questions, arguments, authorities. He participated in the discussions. His opinion was carefully meditated. He delivered it with gravity, and uniformly it was compact, clear, searching, and free from all that was irrelevant, impertinent, or extrinsic. As a matter of course, it was weighty in the deliberations of the court."[22] Such service of an able and industrious judge in conference may be even more valuable than the opinions he writes.

Except in those cases, which are dismissed for want of jurisdiction, or quite obviously require no extended statement of the grounds for the decision, it is the practice of the Supreme Court to hand down opinions in writing which are summarized orally from the bench by the judges who have written them for the Court. The practice of fully stating the case in the opinion has contributed in no slight degree to the influence and prestige of the Supreme Court. While terseness is a virtue too often lacking in judicial opinions, there is no better precaution against judicial mistakes than the setting out accurately and adequately the material facts as well as the points to be decided. The method of the Supreme Court is an example to other courts of the country. For a time, in the early history of the Court, although not at the outset, the practice obtained of having the opinions of the Court delivered by the Chief Justice. Marshall was not responsible for beginning this practice, of which Jefferson bitterly complained. Jefferson objected to an opinion "huddled up in conclave, perhaps by a majority of one, delivered as if unanimous, and with the silent acquiescence of lazy or timid associates, by a crafty chief judge, who sophisticates the law to his mind by the turn of his

[22] 20 Wallace, *Mem.*, X.

own reasoning.'' [23] Jefferson thought there should be a rule requiring the judges to announce *seriatim* their opinions in each case, and thus in a responsible manner take their position.[24] Let every judge, said he, ''throw himself in every case on God and his country; both will excuse him for error and value him for his honesty.'' This practice would be impracticable, but the importance of written opinions as a protection against judicial carelessness and irresponsibility is very great, and no just complaint can be made that the Supreme Court has failed to maintain this safeguard.

At the outset the Supreme Court did not reduce its opinions to writing except in important cases. Dallas probably published all the opinions that were filed. When the Supreme Court assembled in New York at the February term, 1790, only one volume of American reports had appeared. This was Kirby's Cases decided in the Supreme Court of Connecticut, published in 1789 and containing cases from 1758 to 1788. Cranch was the first regular reporter of the Supreme Court of the United States (1801). The practice of delivering opinions in writing had then become the rule, although some cases were omitted. It was not until 1834 that an order was made requiring all opinions to be filed with the clerk, and the manuscript record of the opinions in the clerk's

23 *Letter to Thomas Ritchie,* December 25, 1820; *Jefferson's Works,* Vol. 7, p. 191.

24 *Id., Letter to William Johnson,* March 4, 1823; *Jefferson's Works,* Vol. 7, p. 276.

office begins with the January term, 1835. The printed record does not begin until the December term, 1857.[25]

The practice of writing dissenting opinions began at an early date. There was dissent in *Georgia* v. *Brailsford*,[26] the first case in which opinions were reported. The dissenting opinion of Chief Justice Marshall in *Ogden* v. *Saunders*,[27] a case which dealt with the validity of State insolvent laws, has even been thought by some to be his masterpiece. In their work on the circuits, so long continued, so laborious, and so much discussed, the ablest members of the Court laid themselves open to reversal at the hands of their brethren. The great Chief Justice recorded a dissent in *Bank* v. *Dandridge*,[28] where all the Justices, save himself, concurred in reversing the judgment of the Circuit Court in Virginia, at which Chief Justice Marshall had presided, because of erroneous rulings on questions of law. The opinion of the Court was delivered by Justice Story. In dissenting, the Chief Justice observed: "I should now, as is my custom, when I have the misfortune to differ from this court, acquiesce silently in its opinion, did I not believe that the judgment of the Circuit Court of Virginia gave general surprise to the profession and was generally condemned." [29] In several of such cases, Chief Justice Taney dissented,

[25] J. C. Bancroft Davis, 131 U. S., *Appendix*, XV, XVI.
[26] 2 Dallas 402, 415.
[27] 12 Wheaton, 213, 332.
[28] 12 Wheaton, 64.
[29] *Id.*, 90.

and in one he expressed the difficulty that a judge may have even in construing the opinions of his own court. Seeking in his dissent to justify his dismissal of certain cases at Circuit, the Chief Justice said: "I dismissed them * * * under the impression that I was bound to do so upon the principles upon which this court had decided them in the suits by the trustees. It appears, however, by the opinion just delivered, that I was mistaken, and placed an erroneous construction on the opinions formerly delivered." He did not mean to say that the construction which the majority of the Court put upon its former decisions was not the true one, but that the language used in these decisions "might lead even a careful inquirer to a contrary conclusion!" [30]

There are some who think it desirable that dissents should not be disclosed as they detract from the force of the judgment. Undoubtedly, they do. When unanimity can be obtained without sacrifice of conviction, it strongly commends the decision to public confidence. But unanimity which is merely formal, which is recorded at the expense of strong, conflicting views, is not desirable in a court of last resort, whatever may be the effect upon public opinion at the time. This is so because what must ultimately sustain the court in public confidence is the character and independence of the judges. They are not there simply to decide cases, but to decide them as they think they should be decided, and while it may be regrettable that they cannot always agree,

[30] *Williams v. Gibbs,* 17 Howard, 239, 260.

it is better that their independence should be maintained and recognized than that unanimity should be secured through its sacrifice. This does not mean that a judge should be swift to dissent, or that he should dissent for the sake of self-exploitation or because of a lack of that capacity for cooperation which is of the essence of any group action, whether judicial or otherwise. Independence does not mean cantankerousness and a judge may be a strong judge without being an impossible person. Nothing is more distressing on any bench than the exhibition of a captious, impatient, querulous spirit. We are fortunately free from this in our highest courts in Nation and State, much freer than in some of the days gone by. Dissenting opinions enable a judge to express his individuality. He is not under the compulsion of speaking for the court and thus of securing the concurrence of a majority. In dissenting, he is a free lance. A dissent in a court of last resort is an appeal to the brooding spirit of the law, to the intelligence of a future day, when a later decision may possibly correct the error into which the dissenting judge believes the court to have been betrayed.

Nor is this appeal always in vain. In a number of cases dissenting opinions have in time become the law. In *Rogers* v. *Burlington*,[31] as to validity of municipal bonds, Justices Field, Grier, Miller and Chief Justice Chase dissented and the case was over-

[31] 3 Wallace, 654.

ruled by *Brenham* v. *German American Bank*.[32] In *Doyle* v. *Continental Insurance Company* [33] dealing with the authority of a State to exclude a foreign insurance company from doing business within its borders no matter upon what ground, Justices Bradley, Swayne and Miller dissented. This broad decision was followed in *Security Mutual Life Insurance Company* v. *Prewitt* [34] in which Justices Day and Harlan dissented. Both were recently overruled by a unanimous court in *Terral* v. *Burke Construction Company* [35] in which the Court said that the dissenting opinions in the former cases had now become the law of the Court. This was because the Court found it impossible to sustain the proposition that the authority of a State to exclude a foreign corporation could go so far as to compel it to waive a constitutional right, as for example, to resort to a Federal court. The decision in *Henry* v. *Dick Company*,[36] dealing with restrictions in licenses under patents, a case in which there were three dissents, including that of Chief Justice White, was overruled in the case of *Motion Picture Patents Company* v. *Universal Film Company* [37] and Justices who had carried the Court in the first instance found themselves in

[32] 144 U. S. 173.

[33] 94 U. S. 535.

[34] 202 U. S. 246.

[35] 257 U. S. 529; see also, *Hanover Fire Insurance Co.* v. *Harding*, 272 U. S. 494.

[36] 224 U. S. 1.

[37] 243 U. S. 502.

a minority in the later case.   In *Alpha Cement Company* v. *Massachusetts* [38] there was definite disapproval of what was said by the Court in *Baltic Mining Company* v. *Massachusetts* [39] where Chief Justice White and Justices Van Devanter and Pitney had dissented.   These are illustrations of the victory of dissent, to which may be added the legal tender cases to which I have already referred.   In other instances, where former decisions have not been overruled, dissenting opinions have had a powerful influence on the development of the law.   Dissents in important controversies may be expected because they are cases in which it would be difficult for any body of lawyers freely selected to reach an accord. While the public may not understand division in the Court, because of an illusion as to attainable certitude in opinions as to the law, which is notably absent in other fields, it must be remembered that conviction must have its say and that the conservatism of the Court as a judicial body furnishes all the protection that is needed in the long run against capricious overturning of decisions.

Occasionally, before a decision is reached, a reargument is ordered.   It is not the practice of the Court to give its reasons for ordering another argument, but it is supposed to be due usually, but not always, to an equally divided court, as not infrequently because of the absence or disqualification of a judge cases are heard by less than a full bench.

[38] 268 U. S. 203.
[39] 231 U. S. 68.

After decision has been announced, applications for rehearing are frequent but are very rarely granted. Petitions for rehearing are an improvement on the tavern as counsel may enjoy the luxury of telling the Court to its face what is thought of its opinion, an opportunity which it would be well for counsel generally to forego, exercising a prudent and becoming self restraint. "When the court has made a decision," exclaimed Matt H. Carpenter in closing his argument opposing a motion to set aside a decree,[40] "It is like a decree of Venice, irrevocable; the decision of the Court is the end of the law; God grant the decision may be always right; but right or wrong, it must stand forever." But, as we have seen, the Court sometimes changes its opinion, more often, however, at a later day in deciding another case than in the same case immediately after its decision. On one occasion, Justice Bradley thus answered from the bench, in the course of a colloquy, an application for rehearing: "It ought to be understood, or at least believed, whether it is true or not, that this Court, being a Court of last resort, gives great consideration to cases of importance and involving consequences like this, and there should be a finality somewhere. This custom of making motions for a rehearing is not a custom to be encouraged. It prevails in some States as a matter of ordinary practice to grant a rehearing on a mere application for it, but that practice we do not consider a legitimate one in this Court. It is possible that in the haste of ex-

[40] *Norman v. Bradley,* 12 Wallace, 121.

amining cases before us, we sometimes overlook something, and then we are willing to have that pointed out, but to consider that this Court will re-examine the matter and change its judgment on a case, it seems to me, is not taking a proper view of the functions of this Court. Your application is a proper one to be made, but this matter of motions for rehearing has become — I won't say a nuisance, but very disagreeable to the Court.''

Probably the most argued case on record is that of *Pennsylvania* v. *West Virginia* [41] (1923) with respect to interstate commerce in natural gas, a case which was thrice argued, then decided, and the decision was followed by a rehearing; then three judges dissented from the final decision as they had from the first one, demonstrating that harmony does not always wait on argumentation.

I may mention one interesting incident which the published reports of the court fail to show. I refer to *American Emigrant Company* v. *County of Adams*.[42] The case was argued at the end of November, 1878, and the decision was announced in the middle of the following December. Counsel for appellant filed a petition for rehearing which was denied. Being unconvinced, the appellant retained General Benjamin F. Butler who went into open Court and asked for permission to

[41] 262 U. S. 553, 623; 263 U. S. 350. *Hopt v Utah* came before the Court four times on writs of error, the lower court being reversed three times, but different questions were presented on the hearings; 104 U. S. 631, 110 U. S. 574, 114 U. S. 488, 120 U. S. 430.

[42] 100 U. S. 61.

file a second petition, stating that he was sure that the Court had inadvertently fallen into error and that he was confident that if the Court would take the time to read his petition they would thank him for calling the matter to their attention. Before this, to ask twice for a rehearing was unheard of and it is said that the Court was quick to show its disapproval of the innovation and severe in its criticism of General Butler. But, feeling sure of the justice of his cause, and with his accustomed audacity, he stood his ground, with the result that the minutes of April 14, 1879, show this entry: "On motion of Mr. B. F. Butler it is ordered that the mandate be withheld in this case for the present." The Court then considered the second petition for rehearing and on April 21, 1879, a rehearing was ordered. The case was reargued in the following October and in November the former decision was unanimously reversed.

I have referred to the establishment of tenure during good behavior. It is interesting to observe that of the judges (Chief Justices and Associate Justices) who have served on the Supreme Court since its foundation, exclusive of those now on the bench, twenty-four served less than ten years; sixteen served more than ten years, but less than twenty years; ten served more than twenty years and less than twenty-five years; six served more than twenty-five years and less than thirty years; and eight served more than thirty years. Chief Justice Marshall and Associate Justice Field served over thirty-four years, the latter holding the record by a few months. Justices Story and Harlan served over thirty-three years. The other judges who served over thirty years were Bushrod Washington, William Johnson, McLean and Wayne. Five of the Chief Justices rendered service after they were seventy years of age; Marshall for about ten years and Taney for about seventeen years; Waite for a year and a half; Fuller for seven years; and White for five and a half years. Twenty-three Associate Justices served after they had reached the age of seventy.

While Congress could not provide constitutionally for the compulsory retirement of a judge during good behavior by fixing an age limit, Congress could and did provide [43] (1869) for a voluntary retirement on full pay, at or after the age of seventy when a judge had held his commission for at least ten years. Ten Justices have retired under this Act, including Justice Gray who died before his resignation became effective. On the policy of compelling retirement there are conflicting opinions. Chancellor Kent was compelled to leave the bench at the age of sixty and then at the height of his power proceeded to write his Commentaries. Today we witness the retire\-ment of two judges from the Court of Appeals in New York, and of the Presiding Justice of the Appellate Division of the First Department in that State, in full vigor which permits them to resume the practice of law. The community has no more valuable asset than an experienced judge. It takes

[43] 16 *Statutes at Large,* 45.

a new judge a long time to become completely master of the material of his court. Contrary to general opinion, the work of the court tends to keep a man keen-witted and earnest. Fossilization is not due to the work of the Court but probably to some physical defect which serves to impair mental activity. Doubtless there is a time when a judge reaches, on account of age, the limit of effective service, but it is very difficult to fix that time. We have today the agreeable spectacle of Justice Holmes at eighty-five doing his share of work, or even more, with the same energy and brilliance that he showed twenty years ago. On the other hand, some judges have stayed too long on the bench. An unfortunate illustration was that of Justice Grier who had failed perceptibly at the time of the first argument of the legal tender case. As the decision was delayed he did not participate in it. A committee of the Court waited upon Justice Grier to advise him of the desirability of his retirement and the unfortunate consequences of his being in a position to cast a deciding vote in an important case when he was not able properly to address himself to it. Justice Field tarried too long on the bench. It is extraordinary how reluctant aged judges are to retire and to give up their accustomed work. They seem to be tenacious of the appearance of adequacy. I heard Justice Harlan tell of the anxiety which the Court had felt because of the condition of Justice Field. It occurred to the other members of the Court that Justice Field had served on a committee which waited upon Justice Grier to suggest his retirement, and it was thought that re-calling that to his memory might aid him to decide to retire. Justice Harlan was deputed to make the suggestion. He went over to Justice Field, who was sitting alone on a settee in the robing room apparently oblivious of his surroundings, and after arousing him gradually approached the question, asking if he did not recall how anxious the Court had become with respect to Justice Grier's condition and the feeling of the other Justices that in his own interest and in that of the Court he should give up his work. Justice Harlan asked if Justice Field did not remember what had been said to Justice Grier on that occasion. The old man listened, gradually became alert and finally, with his eyes blazing with the old fire of youth, he burst out:

"Yes! And a dirtier day's work I never did in my life!"

That was the end of that effort of the brethren of the Court to induce Justice Field's retirement; he did resign not long after.

Under present conditions of living, and in view of the increased facility of maintaining health and vigor, the age of seventy may well be thought too early for compulsory retirement. Such retirement is too often the community's loss. A compulsory retirement at seventy-five could more easily be defended. I agree that the importance in the Supreme Court of avoiding the risk of having judges who are unable properly to do their work and yet insist on remaining on the bench, is too great to permit chances to be taken, and any age selected must be somewhat arbitrary as the time of the failing in mental power differs widely. The exigency to be thought of is not illness but decrepitude. Men who take good care of themselves and live the protected and regular life of a judge, are more likely now to be fit at seventy than were their predecessors at sixty-five under the conditions of fifty years ago.

## III

### ACHIEVEMENTS — CEMENTING THE UNION

The Federal Convention did not leave the supremacy of the Constitution, as law binding upon the courts, to implication, however necessary that might be. To remove any possibility of doubt, the Constitution provided: "This Constitution, and the Laws of the United States which shall be made in Pursuance thereof; and all Treaties made, or which shall be made, under the Authority of the United States, shall be the supreme Law of the Land; and the Judges in every State shall be bound thereby, any Thing in the Constitution or Laws of any State to the Contrary notwithstanding."[1] The judicial power of the United States was vested in the Supreme Court, and in such inferior courts as the Congress might establish and this judicial power extends to all cases "arising under this Constitution."[2] It was manifestly impossible that the Supreme Court should appropriately exercise this power in cases arising under the Constitution without sustaining the Constitution as against any legislation that conflicted with it. Instead of the exercise of this authority being a judicial usurpation, the failure to exercise it would have been an unworthy abdication.

I cannot undertake to review the precedents be-

[1] Art. VI. Sec. 2.
[2] Art. III. Secs. 1, 2.

fore the adoption of the Constitution which are frequently cited as early illustrations of the American
doctrine of the duty of courts to apply and thus
maintain what was conceived to be fundamental law;
nor shall I stop to consider the effect of colonial experience in developing an appreciation of the importance of the limitations of government.  For the
present purpose it is enough to say that the idea of
constitutional rights was a natural outgrowth of
colonial life under charters which guaranteed privileges which were cherished and of the conception of
unalienable rights voiced by the Declaration of Independence.  It was an idea which, as I have said,
inhered in the establishment of a Federal government with limited powers.  Professor Beard has
shown us, in his careful analysis of the views of the
members of the Federal Convention, that of twenty-
five members who by reason of character, ability and
assiduity were the dominant element in the Convention, seventeen declared directly or indirectly for
judicial control.[3]  He points out that, in addition to
these, there were several members of minor influence
who seemed to have understood and approved it.[4]
In simple and clear terms the doctrine was stated before ratification of the Constitution by Hamilton in
the Federalist, by Wilson, in Pennsylvania, by Luther Martin, in Maryland, by Marshall, in Virginia,
by Ellsworth, in Connecticut.  Iredell had set it
forth with cogency in North Carolina.

[3] Beard, ''The Supreme Court and the Constitution,'' p. 17.
[4] *Id.*, p. 45.

The question naturally came before the first Congress under the Constitution when it became necessary at once to provide for the organization of the Federal courts and for the definition of the appellate jurisdiction of the Supreme Court. The Judiciary Act of 1789 in definite terms extended this appellate jurisdiction to the review of judgments of State courts involving the validity of a treaty or statute of the United States, or the validity of a statute of a State in the light of the Constitution, treaties and laws of the United States, or involving the construction of the Constitution, treaties and laws of the United States.[5] Very shortly, the Federal circuit courts began to hold State laws invalid when found to be contrary to the Federal Constitution. There were decisions of this sort in 1791, in 1792 and in 1793 before the reported case of *Van Horne's Lessee* v. *Dorrance* [6] (1795) in which Justice Paterson at cir-

[5] Section 25 is as follows: ''That a final judgment or decree in any suit, in the highest court of law or equity of a State in which a decision in the suit could be had, where is drawn in question the validity of a treaty or statute of, or an authority exercised under the United States, and the decision is against their validity; or where is drawn in question the validity of a statute of, or an authority exercised under any State, on the ground of their being repugnant to the constitution, treaties or laws of the United States, and the decision is in favour of such their validity, or where is drawn in question the construction of any clause of the constitution, or of a treaty, or statute of, or commission held under the United States, and the decision is against the title, right, privilege or exemption specially set up or claimed by either party, under such clause of the said Constitution, treaty, statute or commission, may be re-examined and reversed or affirmed in the Supreme Court of the United States. * * * '' 1 Statutes at Large, 85, 86.

[6] 2 Dallas, 304.

cuit held a statute of Pennsylvania invalid as impairing the obligation of a contract. In this opinion, Justice Paterson stated the American doctrine in these words: "Some of the judges in England have had the boldness to assert, that an act of Parliament made against natural equity, is void; but this opinion contravenes the general position, that the validity of an act of Parliament cannot be drawn into question by the judicial department: It cannot be disputed, and must be obeyed. The power of Parliament is absolute and transcendent; it is omnipotent in the scale of political existence. Besides, in England there is no written constitution, no fundamental law, nothing visible, nothing real, nothing certain, by which a statute can be tested. In America the case is widely different: every state in the union has its constitution reduced to written exactitude and precision. What is a Constitution? It is the form of government, delineated by the mighty hand of the people, in which certain first principles of fundamental laws are established. * * * The Constitution fixes limits to the exercise of legislative authority, and prescribes the orbit within which it must move." Referring to the provisions of the declaration of rights of the Constitution of Pennsylvania with respect to freedom of worship and elections by ballot, Justice Paterson continues: "Could the Legislature have annulled these articles, respecting religion, the rights of conscience, and elections by ballot? Surely no. As to these points there was no devolution of power; the authority was purposely withheld, and reserved by the people to themselves. If the Legislature had passed an act declaring, that, in future, there should be no trial by Jury, would it have been obligatory? No: It would have been void for want of jurisdiction, or constitutional extent of power. The right of trial by Jury is a fundamental law, made sacred by the Constitution and cannot be legislated away. * * * I take it to be a clear position; that if a legislative act oppugns a constitutional principle, the former must give way, and be rejected on the score of repugnance. I hold it to be a position equally clear and sound, that, in such case, it will be the duty of the Court to adhere to the Constitution, and to declare the act null and void." [7] In 1796, in *Ware* v. *Hylton*, the Supreme Court of the United States decided that a statute of Virginia was invalid because of its repugnance to the provisions of the treaty of peace with Great Britain.[8]

After the Supreme Court for twenty years had acted under Section 25 of the Judiciary Act in reviewing judgments of State courts, the constitutionality of that section was attacked in *Martin* v. *Hunter's Lessee* [9] (1816) and was sustained in an opinion by Justice Story. The State court had held that Congress had no power to provide for appellate jurisdiction over the State courts and for this reason had refused to obey the mandate of the Supreme Court under a judgment rendered at a preceding

[7] *Id.*, pp. 308, 309.
[8] 3 Dallas, 199.
[9] I Wheaton, 304.

term. Justice Story showed how questions could arise under the Constitution in a State court; as, for example, — "Suppose an indictment for a crime in a state court, and the defendant should allege in his defense that the crime was created by an *ex post facto* act of the state, must not the state court, in the exercise of a jurisdiction which has already rightfully attached, have a right to pronounce on the validity and sufficiency of the defense? * * * It was foreseen that in the exercise of their ordinary jurisdiction, state courts would incidentally take cognizance of cases arising under the constitution, the laws, and treaties of the United States. Yet to all these cases the judical power, by the very terms of the constitution, is to extend. It cannot extend by orignial jurisdiction if that was already rightfully and exclusively attached in the state courts, * * * it must, therefore, extend by appellate jurisdiction, or not at all." [10] While the Constitution operates upon individuals, it also operates upon the States in their corporate capacities. "It is crowded," said Justice Story, "with provisions which restrain or annul the sovereignty of the states in some of the highest branches of their prerogatives. * * * The courts of the United States can, without question, review the proceedings of the executive and legislative authorities of the states, and if they are found to be contrary to the constitution, may declare them to be of no legal validity." [11] The question was put at rest

[10] *Id.*, pp. 341, 342.
[11] *Id.*, pp. 343, 344.

in all its phases by Chief Justice Marshall's opinion a few years later in *Cohens* v. *Virginia* [12] (1821).

It is evident that without the power to maintain the supremacy of the Federal Constitution over State legislation the Constitution would have been a dead letter in some of its most important applications. As Madison said: "I have never been able to see, that without such a view of the subject the Constitution itself could be the supreme law of the land; or that the *uniformity* of the Federal Authority throughout the parties to it could be preserved; or that without this *uniformity*, anarchy & disunion could be prevented." [13] The question could be only as to the repository of the power of declaring repugnant State acts to be void. It could not be given appropriately to the Federal Executive. To have given it to Congress would have been to invite the intrusion of the partiality, passions and uncertainties of politics. It was definitely conferred upon the Supreme Court.

There has been a distinct line of attack upon the authority of the Supreme Court to pass upon the validity of acts of Congress. Mr. Warren's research has established that this power was not seriously challenged until the debate in 1802 on the Circuit Courts' Repeal Act. Prior to that time it appears to have been recognized almost universally "and even in 1802, it was attacked purely on polit-

[12] 6 Wheaton, 264.
[13] Letter of Dec. 1831, to N. P. Trist. Writings of James Madison, Ed. by Gaillard Hunt, Vol. 9, p. 471, [476].

ical grounds and only by politicians from Kentucky, Virginia, North Carolina and Georgia." [14] During the first century of the existence of the Court, the chief conflicts were "over the Court's decisions restricting the limits of State authority and not over those restricting the limits of Congressional power." [15] Federal judges had asserted their authority with respect to the latter from 1792, and the Supreme Court in *Hylton v. United States* [16] (1796), while sustaining the carriage tax there involved had assumed that it was its duty to pass upon the question of constitutionality. Discontent with its decisions arose "*not* because the Court held an Act of Congress unconstitutional, but rather because it refused to do so; the Anti-Federalists and the early Republicans assailed the Court because it failed to hold the Sedition Law, the Bank of the United States charter and the Judiciary Act unconstitutional; the Democrats later attacked the Court for enouncing doctrines which would sustain the constitutionality of an Internal Improvement bill, a voluntary Bankruptcy bill, a Protective Tariff bill and similar measures obnoxious to them; the Federalists equally attacked the Court for refusing to hold unconstitutional the Embargo Act, and the later Republicans assailed it for sustaining the Fugitive Slave Act." [17]

14 Warren, *op. cit.*, Vol. I, p. 256.
15 *Id.*, p. 5.
16 3 Dallas, 171.
17 Warren, *op. cit.*, Vol. I, p. 5.

The Judiciary Act of 1789 assumed that State courts would pass on the validity of acts of Congress and provided for review by the Supreme Court where the State court had held against their validity. In such a case the Supreme Court by the very terms of the act of 1789 was entitled to affirm as well as to reverse the judgment of the State court, and it has consequently been urged that the Judiciary Act recognized the authority of the Supreme Court to declare an act of Congress invalid. Thus Professor Beard says that "it would seem absurd to assume that an act of Congress might be annulled by a state court with the approval of the Supreme Court, but not by the Supreme Court directly." [18] Whether we regard this authority of the Supreme Court as recognized by the Judiciary Act or "as a natural outgrowth of ideas that were common property of the people when the Constitution was framed" we reach the same result. If the limitations of the power of Congress as defined by the Constitution were to be enforced and individual rights were to be protected accordingly, some tribunal must determine when these limitations were exceeded. Naturally it could not be a State tribunal, for that would enable the States to override all Federal authority. The power could not be lodged with the Executive for that would be to make him supreme over Congress. It could not be lodged with Congress for that would make it the sole judge of its own authority and enable it to escape all the limitations of its powers; it

[18] Beard, *op. cit.*, p. 45.

would thus be supreme over the States. If the Constitution as the supreme law was to be applied judicially in the decision of cases or controversies as against State legislation, upon what ground could it be said that it was not to be applied judicially in the decision of cases or controversies as against conflicting acts of Congress? Were the limitations of the Federal Constitution to be maintained as against the States and not as against those possessed of restricted Federal power? And if the judicial power extended to such cases, the determination of the Supreme Court must be final.

By the Supreme Court itself the question was determined in *Marbury* v. *Madison* [19] (1803). The reasoning of Chief Justice Marshall's opinion has never been answered. Said the great Chief Justice: "The powers of the legislature are defined and limited; and that those limits may not be mistaken, or forgotten, the constitution is written. To what purpose are powers limited, and to what purpose is that limitation committed to writing, if these limits may, at any time be passed by those intended to be restrained? * * * It is a proposition too plain to be contested, that the constitution controls any legislative act repugnant to it; or, that the legislature may alter the constitution by an ordinary act. Between these alternatives there is no middle ground. The constitution is either a superior paramount law, unchangeable by ordinary means, or it is on a level with ordinary legislative acts, and, like other acts, is

[19] 1 Cranch, 137.

alterable when the legislature shall please to alter it. * * * If an act of the legislature, repugnant to the constitution, is void, does it, notwithstanding its invalidity, bind the courts, and oblige them to give it effect? * * * It is emphatically the province and duty of the judicial department to say what the law is. * * * So if a law be in opposition to the constitution; if both the law and the Constitution apply to a particular case, so that the court must either decide that case conformably to the law, disregarding the constitution; or conformably to the constitution, disregarding the law; the court must determine which of these conflicting rules governs the case. This is of the very essence of judicial duty.'' [20] The contemporary criticism of the opinion in this case appears to have been directed more to the portion which dealt with the control over cabinet officers than with that which sustained the function of the Court in passing upon the validity of legislation. Jefferson resented Marshall's expression of views relating to the right of the justices of the peace to receive their commissions, questions which under the opinion of the Court were not necessarily involved in the case. With the circumstances out of which that bitter dispute and later controversies arose, with the attacks upon the Court which have been renewed from time to time because of its action in declaring legislation invalid, I shall not attempt to deal. The doctrine of judicial review has been maintained for over one hundred and twenty-three years since *Marbury* v. *Madison*

[20] *Id.*, pp. 176-178.

and practically is as much a part of our system of government as the judicial office itself.

How has this authority of the Court been exercised with respect to acts of Congress. In the seventy years between the adoption of the Constitution and the Civil War, only two acts of Congress were held to be invalid; those under review in *Marbury* v. *Madison* [21] (1803) and in the *Dred Scott* case [22] (1857). Since the Civil War there have been fifty-three decisions of the Supreme Court adjudging the invalidity of acts of Congress.[23] Of these, twenty-three were decided between 1860 and 1900; since the latter year there have been thirty such decisions. In two of these cases, the first legal tender decision and a case relating to the sale of liquor to Indian allottees, the decisions have been overruled and the acts in question held constitutional.[24]

It may be of interest to mention the nature of the decisions holding acts of Congress invalid, classifying them broadly.

Three of these decisions protect the executive department, relating to acts interfering with the

[21] *Id.*

[22] *Scott v. Sandford*, 19 Howard, 393.

[23] Von Moschzisker, "Judicial Review of Legislation" (1923) Addendum I; Bullitt, "The Supreme Court and Unconstitutional Legislation" (1924), Am. Bar Association Journal, Vol. 10, p. 419; Warren, "Congress, the Constitution and the Supreme Court," (1925), pp. 273 *et seq.* This number does not include *Pollard's Lessee v. Hagan*, 3 Howard, 212 (1845) dealing with a private grant.

[24] *Hepburn v. Griswold*, 8 Wallace, 603, overruled by *Knox v. Lee*, 12 Wallace, 457; *Matter of Heff*, 197 U. S. 488, overruled by *United States v. Nice*, 241 U. S. 591.

pardoning power and the power to remove officers.[25] There are eight decisions which may be regarded as protecting the judicial power and the jurisdiction of the courts.[26] Seven others grew out of the amendments to the Constitution following the Civil War. Thus, in *United States v. Reese* [27] (1876) the Court decided that the Fifteenth Amendment conferred authority to legislate as to State elections, only to prevent the denial of the right to vote on account of color, race or previous condition of servitude. (Also, *James v. Bowman* [28] (1903)). In *United States v. Harris* [29] (1882) it was held that the Fourteenth Amendment related only to State action and that so far as the Thirteenth Amendment was concerned the statute in question was broader than the Amendment justified. Later, it was decided that the same statute was not separable so as to be sustained in part. (*Baldwin v. Franks* [30] (1887)). In the *Civil Rights Cases* [31] (1883) it was decided that the provi-

[25] *Ex parte Garland* (1867) 4 Wallace, 333; *United States v. Klein* (1872) 13 Wallace, 128; *Myers v. United States* (1926) 272 U. S. 522.

[26] *Gordon v. United States* (1865) 2 Wallace, 561, 117 U. S. *Appendix*; *The Alicia* (1869) 7 Wallace, 571; *United States v. Evans* (1909) 213 U. S. 297; *Muskrat v. United States* (1911) 219 U. S. 346; *Knickerbocker Ice Co. v. Stewart* (1917) 253 U. S. 149; *Evans v. Gore* (1920) 253 U. S. 245; *Keller v. Potomac Electric Power Co.* (1923) 261 U. S. 428; *Washington v. Dawson & Co.* (1924) 264 U. S. 219.

[27] 92 U. S. 214.

[28] 190 U. S. 127.

[29] 106 U. S. 629.

[30] 120 U. S. 678.

[31] 109 U. S. 3.

sions of the act of March 1, 1875 [32] with respect to the equal enjoyment of the privileges of inns, public conveyances and places of amusement were invalid because of too wide a scope as the Fourteenth Amendment applied only to State action and the Thirteenth Amendment to slavery or involuntary servitude.   In 1913 (*Butts* v. *Merchants Transportation Company*)[33] the court decided that the same act could not be sustained in its operation outside the States, as the provisions of the act with respect to vessels, the District of Columbia and territories, could not be severed from those relating to the States without violating the intent of Congress.   In *Hodges* v. *United States* [34] (1906) it was held that legislation by Congress as to interference with the right of contract, as distinguished from slavery or involuntary servitude, was not authorized by the Thirteenth Amendment.

Twelve decisions may be grouped together as directly supporting the reserved powers of the State. Thus, in *United States* v. *DeWitt* [35] (1870) a provision of an act of Congress was held invalid which attempted to make it a crime to sell a commodity in the States, the act being neither the imposition of a tax nor a regulation of interstate commerce.   In *Collector* v. *Day* [36] (1871) and *United States* v. *Rail-*

[32] 18 Statutes at Large, 335.
[33] 230 U. S. 126.
[34] 203 U. S. 1.
[35] 9 Wallace, 41.
[36] 11 Wallace, 113.

*road Company* [37] (1873), it was decided that Congress could not tax the salaries of State judges or the securities held by a city for municipal purposes. The power to pass a bankruptcy act does not permit an invasion of State authority by making acts .a crime which were independent and not in contemplation of bankruptcy (*United States v. Fox* [38] (1878)). The Trademark Act of 1870 was found to be invalid because it impinged on the power of the States and was not limited to interstate and foreign commerce. (*Trademark Cases* [39] (1879)).  So, the first employers' liability act was beyond the authority of Congress because it was not limited to interstate commerce (1908).[40] In *Coyle* v. *Oklahoma* [41] (1911) it was held that in exercising the power of Congress to admit new States it was necessary to admit them on an equality with the original States.  The child labor acts were held to be unconstitutional, the first (*Hammer* v. *Dagenhart* [42] (1918)) because it was an attempt to control the State in the exercise of the police power over manufacture within the State, and the second (*Bailey* v. *Drexel Furniture Company* [43] (1922)) because it sought to interfere with the authority of the State by the laying of a tax not for revenue but as a penalty for the violation of a regu-

[37] 17 Wallace, 322.
[38] 95 U. S. 670.
[39] 100 U. S. 82.
[40] *The Employers' Liablity Cases*, 207 U. S. 463.
[41] 221 U. S. 559.
[42] 247 U. S. 251.
[43] 259 U. S. 20.

lation outside the scope of Federal power. On a similar ground (*Hill* v. *Wallace*[44] (1922)) a tax on grain involved in contracts for future delivery, imposed by way of penalty, was found to be an invasion of the rights reserved to the States by the Tenth Amendment. Another decision to this effect under the same act of Congress was rendered in *Trusler* v. *Crooks*[45] (1926). The court decided in *Newberry* v. *United States*[46] (1921) that the control over the times, places and manner of holding elections for Senators (Art. I, Sec. 4) did not extend to the processes of nominating candidates. As Justice McReynolds said in delivering the opinion of the court: "The history of the times indicates beyond reasonable doubt that, if the Constitution makers had claimed for this section the latitude we are now asked to sanction, it would not have been ratified."[47] The authority was limited to the election itself.

There have been thirteen decisions which may be broadly classified as holding the provisions of congressional acts invalid because repugnant to the guarantees of personal liberty; that is, with respect to trial by jury, unreasonable searches and seizures, self-incrimination, confrontation of witnesses, liberty of contract, reasonable certainty in defining offenses, and the necessity of a proper hearing in the enforcement of liability to a penalty.[48] In three

[44] 259 U. S. 44.
[45] 269 U. S. 475.
[46] 256 U. S. 232.
[47] *Id.*, p. 256.
[48] *Justices* v. *Murray* (1870) 9 Wallace, 274; *Boyd* v. *United*

other cases acts of Congress have been adjudged invalid as an unconstitutional deprivation of property.[49] The remaining decisions in which congressional acts have been found by the Supreme Court to lie outside the limitations of the legislative power are the income tax case[50] (1895), prior to the Sixteenth Amendment, relating to a tax laid, without apportionment, on the income of property by virtue of ownership; the decisions as to stamp taxes[51] imposed in violation of the prohibition against taxes on articles exported from any State; and the case,[52] (1920) subsequent to the Sixteenth Amendment, invalidating a tax on stock dividends which were not income.

No one can doubt that the exercise of the power to hold invalid State legislation which conflicts with

*States* (1886) 116 U. S. 616; *Callan v Wilson* (1888) 127 U. S. 540; *Counselman v. Hitchcock* (1892) 142 U. S. 547; *Wong Wing v. United States* (1896) 163 U. S. 228; *Kirby v. United States* (1899) 174 U. S. 47; *Rassmussen v. United States* (1905) 197 U. S. 516; *Adair v. United States* (1908) 208 U. S. 161; *Keller v. United States* (1909) 213 U. S. 138; *United States v. L. Cohen Grocery Co.* (1921) 255 U. S. 81; *Weeds, Inc. v. United States* (1921) 255 U. S. 109; *United States v. Moreland* (1922) 258 U. S. 433; *Lipke v. Lederer* (1922) 259 U. S. 557; *Adkins v. Children's Hospital* (1923) 261 U. S. 525.

[49] *Reichart v. Felps* (1868) 6 Wallace, 160; *Monongahela Navigation Co. v. United States* (1893) 148 U. S. 312; *Choate v. Trapp* (1912) 224 U. S. 665.

[50] *Pollock v. Farmers' Loan & Trust Co.*, 157 U. S. 429, 158 U. S. 601.

[51] *Fairbank v. United States* (1901) 181 U. S. 283; *United States v. Hvoslef* (1915) 237 U. S. 1; *Thames & Mersey Ins. Co. v. United States* (1915) 237 U. S. 19.

[52] *Eisner v. Macomber*, 252 U. S. 189.

the Federal Constitution has been a factor of immense importance in cementing the Union. The question has been raised as to the practical value of judicial review of the validity of Federal acts as it has been said that "with the possible exception of the decision in the *Civil Rights Cases*, the integral history of the country would have been little altered had the court not possessed or exercised its power."[53] One of the most distinguished members of the Supreme Court remarked a few years ago that, while he thought "the Union would be imperilled" if the Court could not declare State laws unconstitutional, he did not believe that the United States "would come to an end" if the Court lost its power to declare an Act of Congress void.[54] Such observations undoubtedly have derived support from the infrequency, during a long period, of decisions holding acts of Congress to be invalid and from the fact that few of these cases have been of great importance in shaping the course of the Nation. But the suggestion fails, as it seems to me, to take adequate account of considerations which ought not to be lightly dismissed. The dual system of government implies the maintenance of the constitutional restrictions of the powers of Congress as well as of those of the States. The existence of the function of the Supreme Court is a constant monition to Congress. A judicial, as distinguished from a mere political, solu-

[53] Warren, "The Supreme Court in United States History," Vol. I, p. 16.

[54] Justice Holmes, "The Law and The Court." Speeches of Oliver Wendell Holmes (1913).

tion of the questions arising from time to time has its advantages in a more philosophical and uniform exposition of constitutional principles than would otherwise be probable. Moreover, the expansion of the country has vastly increased the volume of legislative measures and there is severe pressure toward an undue centralization. In Congress, theories of State autonomy, strongly held so far as profession goes, may easily yield to the demands of interests seeking Federal support. Many of our citizens in their zeal for particular measures have little regard for any of the limitations of Federal authority. We have entered upon an era of regulation with a great variety of legislative proposals, constantly multiplying governmental contacts with the activities of industry and trade. These proposals raise more frequently than in the past questions of National, as opposed to State, power. If our dual system with its recognition of local authority in local concerns is worth maintaining, judicial review is likely to be of increasing value. The bill of rights in the Federal Constitution, sustained by the judicial power, must still be regarded as of importance to the liberty of the citizen.

It must be conceded, however, that up to this time, far more important to the development of the country, than the decisions holding acts of Congress to be invalid, have been those in which the authority of Congress has been sustained and adequate national power to meet the necessities of a growing country has been found to exist within constitutional limitations. The vast extension of the exercise of the authority to regulate commerce is a matter of constant comment as we realize how commodious is the edifice erected by the fathers within which the novel intimacies and the undreamed of facilities of our day are conveniently and adequately housed.

The Constitution not only gave to Congress enumerated powers, but it provided that Congress should have authority "To make all Laws which shall be necessary and proper for carrying into Execution the foregoing Powers, and all other Powers vested by this Constitution in the Government of the United States, or in any Department or Officer thereof." [55] This was a grant of vast content. It was an express grant, although in general terms. Its significance was early appraised in *McCulloch* v. *Maryland* [56] (1819) where it was decided that Congress had power to incorporate a bank. That power was not explicitly conferred, but it was not necessary that it should be. It was a power deemed to be essential to the execution of the authority granted. There was found to be no phrase in the Constitution which, like the Articles of Confederation, excluded what were called incidental or implied powers. Chief Justice Marshall was not content with merely deciding the precise point. He was intent on the principles underlying the decision and in the *McCulloch* case, as in others, the logic of the opinion was of far greater importance than its result in the

[55] Art. I, Sec. 8, par. 18.
[56] 4 Wheaton, 316.

instant case. The Chief Justice refuted the argument that the powers of the general government were delegated by the States, which alone were truly sovereign, and must be exercised in subordination to the States which alone possessed supreme dominion. He said that the Convention which framed the Constitution was indeed elected by the State legislatures but that the instrument when it came from their hands was a mere proposal, without obligation, or pretensions to it. It was reported to the existing Congress with the request that it should be submitted to a convention of delegates chosen in each State by the people, under the recommendation of its legislature, for their assent and ratification. He observed that "No political dreamer was ever wild enough  to think of breaking down the lines which separate the States, and of compounding the American people into one common mass." That, of consequence, when they acted they acted in their States, but the measures they adopted did not on that account cease to be the measures of the people themselves or become the measures of the State government. Having established that the government of the Union was a government of the people, and conceding that the government was acknowledged by all to be one of enumerated powers, the Chief Justice asserted, as a proposition commanding universal assent, that this government though limited was supreme within its sphere of action. Although among the enumerated powers the word "bank" or "incorporation" was not found, there were found "the great powers to lay and collect taxes; to borrow money; to regulate commerce; to declare and conduct a war; and to raise and support armies and navies. The sword and the purse, all the external relations, and no inconsiderable portion of the industry of the nation, are entrusted to its government." It might with great reason be contended "that a government entrusted with such ample powers, on the due execution of which the happiness and prosperity of the nation so vitally depends, must also be entrusted with ample means for their execution." * * * The government which has a right to do an act, and has imposed on it the duty of performing that act, must according to the dictates of reason, be allowed to select the means; the Constitution did not leave "to general reasoning" the right of Congress to employ the necessary means. Congress was entitled to make all laws which should be necessary and proper for carrying the powers expressly granted into execution. The Chief Justice found that the word "necessary" did not import "an absolute physical necessity." The word frequently imported no more than that one thing "is convenient, or useful, or essential to another." And, after many illustrations, the Chief Justice arrived at his fundamental principle: "Let the end be legitimate, let it be within the scope of the constitution, and all means which are appropriate, which are plainly adapted to that end, which are not prohibited, but consist with the letter and spirit of the constitution, are constitutional." [57]

As it was found that Congress in this view had authority to incorporate the Bank of the United States it followed that the State within which a branch of that bank was established could not tax it. The power to tax involves the power to destroy, to defeat the power to create. The sovereignty of a State did not extend to those means which are employed by Congress to carry into execution powers conferred upon that body by the people. If the State might tax one instrument employed by the government in the execution of its powers, they might tax every other instrument. They might tax the mail, the mint, patent rights, the papers of the custom-house, judicial process. Hence, the State legislation in question imposing a tax on the Bank of the United States was unconstitutional and void. Thus, the doctrine that Congress could select appropriate means not prohibited by the Constitution to accomplish legitimate ends and that the States could not burden the instrumentalities of the Federal government was placed upon an impregnable foundation.

The decision excited bitter controversy not because the court had assumed to review the authority of Congress to establish the bank, but because the court had held that the act of Congress was constitutional. Madison complained of the breadth of the opinion, saying that "the occasion did not call for

[57] *Id.,* pp. 403-421.

the general and abstract doctrine interwoven with the decision of the particular case"; "it was anticipated," he believed, "by few if any of the friends of the Constitution, that a rule of construction would be introduced as broad & as pliant." [58] But the doctrine and the reasoning which supported it has been approved for more than a hundred years against all criticism. The particular question as to the authority conferred upon the bank was re-examined and the doctrine re-stated and applied in *Osborn* v. *Bank* [59] (1824). There the question was more fully considered of the possession by the corporation of private powers associated with its public authority and the ruling in effect was that although a particular sort of business might not be, when separately considered, within the implied power of Congress, if such business was appropriate or relevant to the banking business the implied power was to be tested by the right to create the bank and the authority to attach to it that which was relevant, in the judgment of Congress, in order to make the business of the bank successful. Following this decision, the Supreme Court sustained the act of Congress (1913) conferring on the Federal Reserve Board the authority to give a special permit to a national bank to act as trustee, executor, administrator or registrar of stocks and bonds (*First National Bank* v. *Fellows* [60]

[58] Letter of Sept. 2, 1819, to Spencer Roane; The Writings of James Madison, Vol. VIII, p. 447, 450.

[59] 9 Wheaton, 738.

[60] 244 U. S. 416.

(1917)). On the same principle rests the validity of the Federal Farm Loan Act of 1916. Undoubtedly the purpose was to facilitate the making of loans upon farm security at low rates of interest. These Federal Land and the Joint Stock banks, however, were established with authority to act as fiscal agents for the government and as depositaries of public moneys and purchasers of government bonds, and this was deemed to bring them within the creative power of Congress; hence Congress could make the farm loan bonds issued by them on the security of farm mortgages and notes exempt as to principal and interest from Federal, State and local taxation. The Court said "that Congress has seen fit, in making these banks fiscal agencies and depositaries of public moneys, to grant to them banking powers of a limited character, in no wise detracts from the authority of Congress to use them for the governmental purposes named, if it sees fit to do so. * * * But whether technically banks, or not, these organizations may serve the governmental purposes declared by Congress in their creation." (*Smith* v. *Kansas City Title & Trust Company* [61] (1920)).

One of the objects of "a more perfect Union" was to "provide for the common defence." [62] A nation which could not fight would be powerless to secure "the Blessings of Liberty to ourselves and our Posterity." We have a *fighting* Constitution. Congress is empowered to declare war, to raise and sup-

[61] 255 U. S. 180.
[62] Constitution, Preamble.

port armies, and to provide and maintain a navy.
To the President was given the direction of war as
the Commander-in-Chief of the Army and Navy.
It was not in the contemplation of the Constitution
that the command of forces and the conduct of campaigns should be in charge of a council, or that as
to this there should be division of authority or responsibility. The prosecution of war demands in
the highest degree the promptness, directness and
unity of action in military operations which alone
can proceed from the Executive. This exclusive
power to command the army and navy and thus to
direct and control campaigns, exhibits, not autoc-
racy, but democracy fighting effectively through
its chosen instruments in accordance with the or-
ganic law. While the President is Commander-in-
Chief, Congress is to prescribe the military organization and to provide the military establishment,
fix numbers, regulate equipment, afford maintenance,
and for these purposes appropriate such sums of
money as it thinks necessary. As a safeguard
against military domination, the power to raise and
support armies is qualified by the provision that ''no
Appropriation of Money to that Use shall be for a
longer Term than two Years''; otherwise this power
is unlimited.[63]

The power to wage war is the power to wage war
successfully. The framers of the Constitution were
under no illusion as to war. They had emerged
from a long struggle which had taught them the

[63] Art. I, Sec. 8, par. 12.

weakness of a mere confederation, and they had no hope that they could hold what they had won save as they established a Union which could fight with the strength of one people under one government entrusted with the common defense. In equipping the national government with the needed authority of war they tolerated no limitations inconsistent with that object, as they realized that the very existence of the Nation might be at stake and that every resource of the people must be at command. Said Madison in the Federalist: "Security against foreign danger is one of the primitive objects of civil society. It is an avowed and essential object of the American Union. The powers requisite for attaining it must be effectually confided to the federal councils." [64] And Hamilton said: "The circumstances that endanger the safety of nations are infinite, and for this reason no constitutional shackles can wisely be imposed on the power to which the care of it is committed." [65] It was in this view that plenary authority was given to Congress to wage war. It is also in the light of this conception of national exigencies that we must read the provision already quoted under which Congress has authority to make all the laws that may be needed to execute the powers vested in the national government. It remained, however, for the Great War to furnish the occasion for decisions of the Supreme Court sustaining this authority in its broadest scope. The

[64] *Federalist*, No. XLI.
[65] *Federalist*, No. XXIII.

Selective Draft Act of 1917 was held to be constitutional.[66] Chief Justice White, in delivering the opinion in these cases, said that "the very conception of a just government and its duty to the citizen" included "the reciprocal obligation of the citizen to render military service in case of need and the right to compel it."[67] To the framers of the Constitution the draft was a familiar mode of raising armies, as it had been resorted to by the Colonies to fill up their quotas in the Revolutionary War. The draft was put in force both by the Union and by the Confederacy during the Civil War and its validity was sustained in both North and South. Lincoln had strongly argued for it. Said he: "It is not a power to raise armies if State authorities consent; nor if the men to compose the armies are entirely willing; but it is a power to raise and support armies given to Congress by the Constitution, without an 'if'."[68] The Supreme Court found no difficulty in following the same reasoning.

The power exercised by the President in time of war has been greatly augmented, outside of his function as Commander-in-Chief, through legislation increasing his administrative authority. War demands the highest degree of efficient organization, and Congress in the nature of things cannot pre-

[66] *Arver v. United States* [Selective Draft Law Cases], 245 U. S. 366; *Goldman v. United States*, 245 U. S. 474; *Ruthenberg v. United States*, 245 U. S. 480.

[67] 245 U. S. p. 378.

[68] "Complete Works," Nicolay and Hay, (Century Co.) Vol. IX, p. 77.

scribe many important details as it legislates for the purpose of meeting the exigencies of war. The principles governing the delegation of legislative power are clear, and while they are of the utmost importance, they are not such as to make the appropriate exercise of legislative power impracticable. Congress cannot be permitted to abandon to others its essential legislative functions; but in time of war when legislation must be adapted to many situations of the utmost complexity, there is special need for flexibility and for every resource of practicality. The breadth of the power which may thus be conferred upon the President, and exercised by him through officers whom he vests with authority under the congressional sanction, is well illustrated in the recent decision of the Supreme Court in *United States* v. *Chemical Foundation* [69] (1926) with respect to the disposition of the property of alien enemies which had been seized. By virtue of its incidental powers in the prosecution of the war, Congress took over the railroads of the country and was held to be entitled to fix the rates on intrastate traffic, overriding the State power over that subject (*Northern Pacific Railway Company* v. *North Dakota*).[70] The action of Congress was also sustained in taking possession and control of telephone and telegraph lines, and the Supreme Court decided that whether the exercise of the power conferred upon the President by Congress in the Joint Resolution of July

[69] 272 U. S. 1.
[70] 250 U. S. 135.

16, 1918, was justified by the conditions at the time, or was actuated by proper motives, were questions relating to the executive discretion and were not within the cognizance of the judiciary (*Dakota Central Telephone Company* v. *South Dakota*).[71] A few weeks ago the Supreme Court determined that the war powers of Congress embraced the authority to require that a corporation on proper demand should make delivery of new certificates of stock to the Alien Property Custodian or his depositaries covering shares standing in the names of or held for enemies, without the surrender of the original certificates (*Great Northern Railway Company* v. *Sutherland*).[72]

It was under the war power of Congress that the War-time Prohibition Act, approved ten days after the signing of the armistice with Germany, was upheld. Notwithstanding the cessation of hostilities, the Armistice did not abridge or suspend the power to Congress to resort to prohibition of the liquor traffic as a means of increasing war efficiency (*Hamilton* v. *Kentucky Distilleries Company*,[73] *Ruppert* v. *Caffey*).[74] It was in the case last cited that Justice Brandeis suggested that "some confusion of thought might perhaps have been avoided, if, instead of distinguishing between powers by the terms express and implied, the terms specific and general had been

[71] 250 U. S. 163.
[72] 273 U. S. 182.
[73] 251 U. S. 146.
[74] 251 U. S. 264, 301.

used," for the power conferred to make all laws which shall be necessary and proper for carrying into execution powers specifically enumerated "is also an express power." He re-asserted, in what may be regarded as an extreme application of the war power, the Marshall doctrine that while this is a government of enumerated powers it has full attributes of sovereignty within the limits of those powers.

But it was recognized that the war power of the United States, like its other powers and like the police power of the States, is subject to applicable constitutional limitations. (*Hamilton* v. *Kentucky Distilleries Co.*).[75] Thus the exercise of this power is subject to the Fifth and Sixth Amendments. This was decided in the celebrated case of Milligan[76] (1866). He was a citizen of Indiana, who had been tried by a military commission at Indianapolis on a charge of aiding the enemy and conspiring against the Government, and had been sentenced to be hanged. He was not a resident of one of the rebellious States, nor a prisoner of war and he had not been in the military or naval service. It was conceded that in the place where actual military operations are being conducted the ordinary rights of citizens must yield to paramount military necessity. But a different question with respect to the rights of citizens, and others not enemies, was presented in places which were outside the actual theatre of war. The

[75] 251 U. S. 146.
[76] 4 Wallace, 2.

Court in Milligan's case was unanimous in the opinion that under the terms of the Act of Congress creating the commission it had no jurisdiction in the particular case, but the majority of the Court went further and declared that Congress was without power to provide for the trial of citizens by military commissions save in the locality of actual war and when there was no access to the courts, maintaining with eloquent emphasis the guarantees of freedom contained in the Fifth and Sixth Amendments. ''The Constitution of the United States, said the opinion, is a law for rulers and people, equally in war and in peace, and covers with the shield of its protection all classes of men, at all times, and under all circumstnces.'' The majority of the Court asserted that ''martial law cannot arise from a *threatened* invasion. The necessity must be actual and present; the invasion real, such as effectually closes the courts and deposes the civil administration. * * * Martial rule can never exist where the courts are open, and in the proper and unobstructed exercise of their jurisdiction. It is also confined to the locality of actual war.''[77] The minority of four Justices, led by Chief Justice Chase, while agreeing that there was no jurisdiction in Milligan's case under the Act of Congress, strongly insisted that Congress in time of war had power to provide for the punishment of citizens, charged with conspiracy against the United States, by military tribunals, if it was deemed necessary for the public welfare. The great importance of the

[77] *Id.*, p. 127.

ruling of the majority in maintaining the reasonable freedom of the citizen and his right to normal judicial procedure in time of war is apparent. On similar grounds, constitutional rights of property, aside from the unavoidable deprivations which take place where the conflict rages, must be respected and for those takings, although for military purposes, which are deliberate appropriations, just compensation must be made (*United States* v. *Russell* [78] (1871)). The Supreme Court has also held that the existence of a state of war does not suspend the guarantees of the Constitution as to personal liberty so as to justify legislation creating crimes by wholly indefinite terms and without setting up any ascertainable standard of guilt. (*United States* v. *Cohen Grocery Co.* [79] (1921)).

The Supreme Court has sustained the power of the United States to acquire territory and the authority of Congress to govern it. The extraordinary division of the court in the *Insular* cases [80] (1901) in which Justice Brown anounced the conclusion and judgment of the court, although the judges who concurred with him and made the judgment possible disagreed with the views expressed in his opinion, and four Judges dissented from the judgment, did not represent a cleavage that was destined to endure. From the conflict of views with respect to the status of the possessions which were acquired as a result

[78] 13 Wallace, 623.

[79] 255 U. S. 81. For decisions under the *Espionage Act* of June 15, 1917 (40 Statutes at Large, 219). See *infra*, pp. 164 *et seq.*

[80] 182 U. S. 244.

of the war with Spain, the view expressed by Justice White in the earlier cases came to be the dominant one, as set forth by him in the opinion delivered for the court in *Rassmussen* v. *United States* [81] (1904). It may thus be regarded as established that territory may be acquired without incorporating it into the United States as an integral part, that Congress may govern acquired territory without being under obligation to enact therefor a system of laws which shall include the right of trial by jury, and that the Constitution does not without legislation and of its own force carry such right to the territory so situated. Congress is to determine when the territory shall be incorporated into the United States. The result of the decisions as to our insular possessions is strongly to confirm the national power.

The treaty-making power is essential to a nation. It is conferred by the Constitution without express limitations. The President is authorized "by and with the Advice and Consent of the Senate, to make Treaties, provided two-thirds of the Senators present concur." [82] It is a power in no sense reserved in any particular to the States. Much of the discussion as to the breadth of the power is academic as relating to hypothetical cases which never would arise in fact. The treaty-making power should be considered as broad enough to cover all subjects that properly pertain to our foreign relations. The decisions of the Supreme Court, however, leave much to be

[81] 197 U. S. 516.
[82] Art. II, Sec. 2, par. 2.

determined. In *Geofroy* v. *Riggs* [83] (1890) the Court said: "That the treaty power of the United States extends to all proper subjects of negotiation between our government and the governments of other nations, is clear. * * * The treaty power, as expressed in the Constitution, is in terms unlimited except by those restraints which are found in that instrument against the action of the government or of its departments, and those arising from the nature of the government itself and of that of the States. It would not be contended that it extends so far as to authorize what the Constitution forbids, or a change in the character of the government or in that of one of the States, or a cession of any portion of the territory of the latter, without its consent. * * * But with these exceptions, it is not perceived that there is any limit to the questions which can be adjusted touching any matter which is properly the subject of negotiation with a foreign country." With reference to the cession of territory by the United States it may be recalled that it was said in *Lattimer* v. *Poteet* (1840) that it was "a sound principle of national law, and applies to the treaty-making power of this government, whether exercised with a foreign nation or an Indian tribe, that all questions of disputed boundaries may be settled by the parties to the treaty." [84]

When the treaty with Great Britain of 1916, providing for the protection of migratory birds in the

[83] 133 U. S. 258, 266.
[84] 14 Peters, 4, 14.

United States and Canada, was before the Supreme
Court it was alleged on behalf of the State of Missouri that the statute passed pursuant to the engage-
ment of the treaty was an unconstitutional interference with the powers reserved to the States by the
Tenth Amendment. It had already been held in the
lower Federal courts, prior to the treaty, that Congress could not regulate the killing of migratory
birds within the States, and it was argued that a
treaty was subject to the limitations of the Constitution; that one limitation was that "what an act
of Congress could not do unaided, in derogation of
the powers reserved to the States, a treaty cannot
do." The Supreme Court said in reply to this contention: "Acts of Congress are the supreme law of
the land only when made in pursuance of the Constitution, while treaties are declared to be so when
made under the authority of the United States. It
is open to question whether the authority of the
United States means more than the formal acts
prescribed to make the convention. We do not mean
to imply that there are no qualifications to the treaty-
making power; but they must be ascertained in a
different way. It is obvious that there may be matters of the sharpest exigency for the national well
being that an act of Congress could not deal with
but that a treaty followed by such an act could, and
it is not lightly to be assumed that, in matters requiring national action, 'a power which must belong
to and somewhere reside in every civilized government' is not to be found. * * * we may add that

when we are dealing with words that also are a con-
stituent act, like the Constitution of the United
States, we must realize that they have called into
life a being the development of which could not have
been foreseen completely by the most gifted of its
begetters. It was enough for them to realize or to
hope that they had created an organism; it has taken
a century and  has cost their successors much sweat
and blood to prove that they created a nation.  The
case before us must be considered in the light of our
whole experience and not merely in that of what was
said a hundred years ago.  The treaty in question
does not contravene any prohibitory words to be
found in the Constitution.  The only question is
whether it is forbidden by some invisible radiation
from the general terms of the Tenth Amendment.''
The court found that it was not.  ''No doubt the
great body of private relations usually fall within
the control of the State, but a treaty may override
its power.  We do not have to invoke the later devel-
opments of constitutional law for this proposition;
it was recognized as early as *Hopkirk* v. *Bell,*
3 Cranch, 454, with regard to statutes of limitation,
and even earlier, as to confiscation, in *Ware* v. *Hylton,* 3 Dall. 199.  It was assumed by Chief Justice
Marshall with regard to the escheat of land to the
State in *Chirac* v. *Chirac,* 2 Wheat. 259, 275.'' [85]
From this recent statement of the broad principle
it may be concluded that while through treaties it
would be impossible to change the structure of our

[85] *Missouri v. Holland* (1920) 252 U. S. 416, 433.

government, the treaty-making power extends to all questions that are appropriately dealt with in dealings between nations and in the peaceful adjustment of international controversies. Former President Taft has expressed the view that the treaty-making power is dealing with our foreign relations, "and when we deal with our foreign relations, we are a nation undivided and presenting a united front. Everything, therefore, that is natural or customarily involved in such foreign relations, a treaty may cover, whether beyond the law-making power of Congress and within the control of state legislatures, or not." [86]

It is recognized by the Supreme Court that a treaty may repeal a law of Congress, if it is inconsistent with it, and a law of Congress may repeal a treaty.[87] It is important to note that the repeal of a treaty by Congress does not end it as an international contract. It merely repeals the treaty as municipal law, leaving the Nation to meet its international obligations.

As the Supreme Court has buttressed the essential national power, it has also recognized that as a Nation we are one of a community of civilized nations and as such we are subject to the obligations of international law. The term international law designates "the principles and rules of conduct which States feel themselves bound to observe, and therefore, do commonly observe in their relations with

[86] Taft, *Our Chief Magistrate and his Powers*, p. 110,
[87] *United States v. Payne*, 264 U. S. 446.

each other.'' The Constitution empowers Congress to punish ''Offenses against the Law of Nations.'' [88] This is a recognition of the law of nations. International law is our law. As early as the case of the *Nereide* [89] Chief Justice Marshall said: ''Till such an act'' (referring to action by Congress with reference to the question before the court) ''be passed, the Court is bound by the law of nations which is a part of the law of the land.'' In this view the Supreme Court has decided that Congress could enact a law to provide for the punishment of the offense of counterfeiting the notes of a foreign bank or corporation. The Court was of the opinion that the counterfeiting of foreign securities, whether national or corporate, was an offense against the law of nations and because of the duty of the United States to protect a right secured by the law of nations to another nation or its people, Congress could prescribe punishment (*United States* v. *Arjona*,[90] (1887). ''International law,'' said the Court, through Justice Gray in *The Paquete* v. *Habana* [91] (1899) ''is part of our law, and must be ascertained and administered by the courts of justice of appropriate jurisdiction, as often as questions of right depending upon it are duly presented for their determination. For this purpose, where there is no treaty, and no controlling executive or legislative

[88] Art. I, Sec. 8, par. 10.
[89] 9 Cranch, 388, 423.
[90] 120 U. S. 479.
[91] 175 U. S. 677, 700.

act or judicial decision, resort must be had to the customs and usages of civilized nations; and, as evidence of these, to the works of jurists and commentators, who by years of labor, research and experience, have made themselves peculiarly well acquainted with the subjects of which they treat. Such works are resorted to by judicial tribunals, not for the speculations of their authors concerning what the law ought to be, but for trustworthy evidence of what the law really is.''

International law rests upon the consent of civilized nations with respect to the principles and rules governing their intercourse. It is not the law of a particular State save as it is the law of all States. Where Congress within its competency establishes a rule, the Supreme Court must enforce it even if it override a treaty or is inconsistent with international law, but in the absence of such a provision of our municipal law, international law will be applied to a case within its purview. As resort is had in all countries to the writings of jurists and to judicial decisions in determining what is international law, the Supreme Court of the United States is of high authority not only in applying that law but as its expositor.

## IV

## The States and the Nation

"The Constitution, in all its provisions," said Chief Justice Chase in *Texas* v. *White* (1869) "looks to an indestructible Union, composed of indestructible States."[1] The only restriction at present on the power of amending the Constitution is that no State without its consent shall be deprived of its equal suffrage in the Senate.[2] The powers not delegated to the United States by the Constitution, nor prohibited by it to the States, are reserved to the States respectively, or to the people.[3]

At the very beginning, when suit was brought in the Supreme Court against the State of Georgia[4] by a citizen of another State, the State refused to appear. Georgia had already availed herself of the original jurisdiction of the Supreme Court to bring suit,[5] but denied that she could be made a defendant against her will at the suit of an individual. Hamil-

[1] 7 Wallace, 700, 725.

[2] Art. V. This Article also provided that no amendment which might be made prior to 1808 should affect the first and fourth clauses in the ninth section of the first Article, that is, the clauses with respect to the migration or importation of such persons as any of the States then existing should think proper to admit and as to direct taxes.

[3] Tenth Amendment.

[4] *Chisholm v. Georgia* (1792), 2 Dallas, 419.

[5] *Georgia v. Brailsford*, 2 Dallas, 402.

ton, Madison and Marshall had declared in advance of ratification of the Constitution that such a suit against a State would not lie. Hamilton had said: "To what purpose would it be to authorize suits against States for the debts they owe? How could recoveries be enforced? It is evident that it could not be done without waging war against the contracting State; and to ascribe to the federal courts, by mere implication, and in destruction of a pre-existing right of the State governments, a power which would involve such a consequence, would be altogether forced and unwarrantable." [6] Madison in Virginia had said: "It is not in the power of individuals to call any state into court." [7] The decision to the contrary in *Chisholm* v. *Georgia* [8] astonished the country and caused intense feeling. All the States were greatly indebted and "to quiet the apprehensions that were so extensively entertained" [9] the Eleventh Amendment was adopted. This Amendment, declared in force in 1798, provided that "the Judicial Power of the United States shall not be construed to extend to any suit in law or equity, commenced or prosecuted against one of the United States by Citizens of another State, or by Citizens or Subjects of any Foreign State." It remained for the Supreme Court to decide, as it did in 1890,[10] that

[6] *Federalist,* No. LXXXI.

[7] 3 Elliot's Debates, 533. As to Marshall's views, see 3 Elliot's Debates, 555, Beveridge's Marshall, Vol. I, p. 454.

[8] 2 Dallas, 419.

[9] Marshall, C. J., in *Cohens* v. *Virginia* (1821), 6 Wheaton, 264, 406.

[10] *Hans* v. *Louisiana,* 134 U. S. 1.

a State could not be sued by one of its own citizens without its consent. Justice Bradley in delivering the opinion in that case took the view that the decision in *Chisholm* v. *Georgia* was wrong, but this was afterwards said to be an expression *obiter* and not binding upon the Court.[11] The Eleventh Amendment cannot be evaded successfully by allowing the name of a State to be used by its citizens, where the State is without actual interest, in a suit against another State.[12] Where, however, the owner of bonds of North Carolina made an absolute gift of some of them to South Dakota, that State was held entitled to sue North Carolina and obtain judgment.[13] The right of the United States to sue a State has been sustained as being within the spirit of the Constitution although not conferred by its letter.[14]

Because a State may not be sued by an individual, it does not follow that persons are remediless when State officers seek to enforce unconstitutional laws of the State. Chief Justice Marshall held that the State Auditor of Ohio was amenable to suit when he was proceeding under an invalid tax law of the State to interfere with Federal authority.[15] It has come to be well settled, after much discussion in several cases, that suit will lie in the Federal courts to en-

---

[11] *South Dakota v. North Carolina* (1904), 192 U. S. 286, 318.

[12] *New Hampshire v. Louisiana* (1883), 108 U. S. 76.

[13] *South Dakota v. North Carolina* (1904), 192 U. S. 286.

[14] *United States v. North Carolina* (1890), 136 U. S. 211; *United States v. Texas* (1892), 143 U. S. 621; *United States v. Michigan* (1903), 190 U. S. 379.

[15] *Osborn v. Bank of the United States* (1824), 9 Wheaton, 738.

join State officials from executing laws charged to
be in violation of the Federal Constitution when
these officials are clothed with some duty in regard to
the enforcement of the laws of the State and have
threatened or are about to begin proceedings.[16]   In
this way the validity of State regulation of the rates
of railroads and other public service corporations
alleged to be confiscatory has been contested.   The
theory is that the defendant officers in such cases
are wrongdoers charged to be acting without the
authority of a valid law.   The same principle extends to Federal officials.   Thus, with respect to
the homestead of Robert E. Lee at Arlington, the
Supreme Court decided that although the title
was asserted to be in the United States, suit could be
brought against the Federal officers in possession to
determine whether the title was valid.[17]   Another
illustration is that of a suit against the Secretary of
War to pass upon the validity of his action in establishing harbor lines as it was asserted that by an
unauthorized act he had wrongfully interfered with
the property rights of the plaintiff.[18] But a State,
and of course the United States, is protected from
suit brought by an individual either against it or
against its officers where they represent the government's action and liability and are not charged with
proceeding without valid authority.   And this principle holds good although the State has taken over the

[16] *Ex parte Young* (1907), 209 U. S. 123.
[17] *United States v. Lee* (1882), 106 U. S. 196.
[18] *Philadelphia Co. v. Stimson* (1912), 223 U. S. 605.

conduct of a business of a private character.   The
fact that, in an undertaking of this sort, the limitation as to Federal taxation of the instrumentalities
of a State may not be applicable[19] does not make the
State subject to suit.[20]  That the rulings to which I
have referred, with respect to the suability of State
officers to restrain unconstitutional action, has not
impaired the essential immunity of the State from
suit by individuals, is shown by the recent decision of
the Supreme Court in issuing a writ of prohibition
to the Federal District Court against entertaining at
suit *in personam* against the Superintendent of Public Works of the State of New York.[21]  He was sued
in his official capacity for damages due to the operation of tugs on the Erie Canal in the course of his
duty, and liability, if any, would have rested on the
people of the State in their public and corporate
capacity.

The original jurisdiction of the Supreme Court
over controversies between States is exclusive, as
in its nature it must be.   No State may enter into
any treaty, alliance or confederation.   No State,
without the consent of Congress, can keep troops, or
ships of war in time of peace, enter into any agreement or compact with another State, or with a foreign power, or engage in war, unless actually invaded
or in such imminent danger as will not admit of
delay.[22]  The Supreme Court has referred with ap-

[19] *South Carolina v. United States* (1905), 199 U. S. 437.
[20] *Murray v. Wilson Distilling Co.* (1909), 213 U. S. 151.
[21] *Ex parte New York* (1921), 256 U. S. 490.
[22] Art. I. Sec. 10.

parent approval to Justice Story's view that the first clause of Section 10 of Article I applies "to treaties of a political character, such as treaties of alliance for purposes of peace and war; and treaties of confederation, in which the parties are leagued for mutual government, political cooperation, and the exercise of political sovereignty and treaties of cession of sovereignty; or conferring internal political jurisdiction, or external political dependence, or general commercial privileges"; while "compacts and agreements" (in the third clause) might be applied "to such as regarded what might be deemed mere private rights of sovereignty; such as questions of boundaries; interests in land situate in the territory of each other; and other internal regulations for the mutual comfort and convenience of states bordering on each other." [23] Where an independent and sovereign State could seek a remedy by negotiation, and that failing, by force, the States of the United States have formed a permanent Union of peace, with a permanent court of justice to which their controversies may be brought for final determination. Diplomatic powers and the right to make war having been surrendered to the general government, it was necessary to find a remedy and that is given in the constitutional provisions as to the judicial power. Disputes over international boundaries have frequently led to war. We have had many grave disputes over boundaries between the States and they have been settled through the original jurisdiction

[23] *Kansas v. Colorado* (1902), 185 U. S. 125, 140; 2 *Story on the Constitution*, Secs. 1402, 1403.

of the Supreme Court. But the exercise of this jurisdiction, clearly conferred and vital as it was, did not escape the most earnest challenge by the States. In the case of *New Jersey* v. *New York*,[24] the Supreme Court decided that if the defendant did not appear the Court would proceed to hear the cause on behalf of the complainant and to render its decree. Massachusetts resisted determinedly the suit of Rhode Island to establish the northern boundary between the States. Massachusetts called to her aid the eloquence of Webster in a motion to dismiss for want of jurisdiction, but without avail.[25] In 1849, the Supreme Court brought to an adjustment the disputed limits between Missouri and Iowa,[26] a controversy which had been so bitter that troops on each side had been called out. "In Europe," said Senator Cass referring to this case, "armies run lines, and they run them with bayonets and cannon. They are marked with ruin and devastation. In our country they are run by an order of this Court. They are run by an unarmed surveyor, with his chain and his compass, and the monuments which he puts down are not monuments of devastation, but peaceable ones."[27] Since, then, questions relating to territorial jurisdiction between Florida and Georgia, Alabama and Georgia, Virginia and West Virginia, South Carolina and Georgia, Indiana and

[24] (1831), 5 Peters, 284; see *New York v. Connecticut* (1799), 4 Dallas, 1.

[25] *Rhode Island v. Massachusetts* (1838), 12 Peters, 657.

[26] 7 Howard, 660.

[27] Cong. Globe, 33d Cong., 2d Sess. 298.

Kentucky, Iowa and Illinois, Nebraska and Iowa, Virginia and Tennessee, Louisiana and Mississippi, Arkansas and Tennessee, Oklahoma and Texas, New Mexico and Colorado, Michigan and Wisconsin, and Massachusetts and New York have been brought before the Court.[28] In *Oklahoma* v. *Texas,* the Court found it necessary to appoint a receiver whose important activities were under its direct control.

Not only questions of territory are thus decided but one State may sue another to recover the amount of a debt. But how was a money judgment to be enforced? I have already referred to the suit of South Dakota to recover upon North Carolina bonds. In that case, it was recognized that the Court was encountering a serious difficulty. "We are confronted," said the Court, "with the contention that there is no power in this Court to enforce such a judgment, and such lack of power is conclusive evidence that, notwithstanding the general language of the Constitution, there is an implied exception of actions brought to recover money." It was observed that the public property held by any municipality, county or state is exempt from seizure upon execution, because it is held in trust for public purposes. "We have, then," continued the Court, "on the one hand the general language of the Constitution vesting jurisdiction in this Court over 'controversies between two or more States,' the history of that juris-

[28] 17 Howard, 478; 23 Howard, 505; 11 Wallace, 39; 93 U. S. 4; 136 U. S. 479; 143 U. S. 359; 147 U. S. 1; 158 U. S. 267; 202 U. S. 1; 246 U. S. 158; 252 U. S. 372; 258 U. S. 574; 267 U. S. 30; 268 U. S. 252; 270 U. S. 295; 271 U. S. 65.

dictional clause in the convention, the cases of *Chisholm* v. *Georgia, United States* v. *North Carolina,* and *United States* v. *Michigan* (in which this Court sustained jurisdiction over actions to recover money from a State,) the manifest trend of other decisions, the necessity of some way of ending controversies between States, and the fact that this claim for the payment of money is one justiciable in its nature; on the other, certain expression of individual opinions of justices of this court, the difficulty of enforcing a judgment for money against a State, by reason of its ordinary lack of private property subject to seizure upon execution, and the absolute inability of a court to compel a levy of taxes by the legislature.'' The Court found a way to avoid a determination of the question.[29] But the controversy over the indebtedness of West Virginia to Virginia presented the issue in an unescapable fashion. Virginia sought an adjudication of the amount due from West Virginia as its equitable proportion of the public debt of Virginia which West Virginia had assumed at the time of its creation as a State. The Supreme Court took jurisdiction,[30] and reviewing the transactions between the States gave its decision as to the basis of liability.[31] It became necessary to appoint a Master to determine particular questions and, on the coming in of his report, the Court entered a decree [32] against West Virginia for over twelve millions of dollars,

[29] *South Dakota v. North Carolina* (1904), 192 U. S. 286, 318, 320.
[30] (1907) 206 U. S. 290.
[31] (1911) 220 U. S. 1.
[32] (1915) 238 U. S. 202.

with interest, as its equitable proportion of the debt.
West Virginia petitioned for a writ of *mandamus* to
compel the levy of a tax by the legislature of West
Virginia to pay the amount due under the decree.
Chief Justice White, speaking for the Court,[33] regarded it as elementary that "judicial power essentially involves the right to enforce the results of its
exertion"; this applied to the exercise of the power
in controversies between the States.  Referring to
the doubt which had been raised in the opinion in
*South Dakota* v. *North Carolina*, the Chief Justice
said that the question of the power to enter judgment against West Virginia had been foreclosed by
its rendition.  Both parties admitted that West Virginia had no property not used for governmental
purposes and therefore the judgment was not susceptible of enforcement through a writ of execution
if such property could not be taken.  The experience
of the Colonies was reviewed and it was shown that
the absence of power in the Confederation "to control the governmental attributes of the states for
the purpose of enforcing findings concerning disputes between them gave rise to most serious consequences and brought the states to the very verge
of physical struggle and resulted in the shedding of
blood, and would, if it had not been for the adoption
of the Constitution have rendered nugatory the
great results of the Revolution."  And on consideration of the purposes of the Constitution the Court
found that it could not escape the conclusion that as

[33] (1918) 246 U. S. 565, 591-593, 598, 599, 601-603.

the State as a governmental entity had been subjected
to the judicial power, the duty of enforcing the judgment was certain even though resort to appropriate
remedies operated on the governmental powers of
the State. What then were the appropriate remedies? The Chief Justice concluded that Congress,
having complete control over agreements between
States, had plenary power to provide for the execution of such contracts; that Congress had authority
to legislate for the enforcement of the obligation of
West Virginia and that this authority extended to
the creation of new remedies. To treat the power
of Congress to legislate to secure the performance
by a State of its duty under the Constitution as coercion comes "back at last to the theory that any one
State may throw off and disregard without sanction
its obligation and subjection to the Constitution," a
conclusion which would be to disregard the very principles which led to the carving out of West Virginia
from the territory of Virginia; that is "to disregard
and overthrow the doctrines irrevocably settled by
the great controversy of the Civil War, which in
their ultimate aspect find their consecration in the
Amendments to the Constitution which followed."
This, — from the lips of one who in his youth had
fought to maintain the Confederacy but as Chief
Justice exemplified the loftiest statesmanship and
patriotic devotion to a united country. The Court
refrained from passing on further questions as, having established the right judicially to enforce the
judgment against the State and its governmental

agencies, and the power of Congress to legislate for
that purpose, the Court was fain to believe that it
would be spared the necessity of exercising its power
against one of the States to compel it to discharge
a plain duty resting upon it under the Constitution.
This belief proved to be well founded. A motion
made by Virginia for the appointment of a receiver
was denied,[34] and a year later an acknowledgment
of the satisfaction of the Court's decree was presented and filed.[35]

The Supreme Court has indicated that notwithstanding the general language of the Constitution it
does not follow that the Court would have jurisdiction in all cases where one State chose to make complaint against another, no matter what the subject
or the nature of the injury. The general language
used by Chief Justice Marshall in *Cohens* v. *Virginia*[36] has been modified to some extent in later
cases. Thus, jurisdiction was denied when private
persons were seeking to use the name of the State
to enforce their rights and the State had no real interest.[37] Despite the letter of the Constitution as to
suits brought by a State against the citizens of
another State, when suit was brought to enforce the
penal laws of one State against the citizens of another, the Court refused to take jurisdiction.[38] Again,

[34] April, 1919.

[35] March, 1920.

[36] (1821) 6 Wheaton, 264, 393; *Missouri v. Illinois* (1901), 180
U. S. 208, 240.

[37] *New Hampshire v. Louisiana* (1883), 108 U. S. 76.

[38] *Wisconsin v. Pelican Insurance Co.* (1888), 127 U. S. 265.

when although one State sued another a controversy between them was not actually presented, the action complained of being the alleged unauthorized conduct of a health officer, the Court dismissed the bill, although it may be regarded that relief, rather than jurisdiction, was denied.[39] In that case, Chief Justice Fuller said that "in order that a controversy between States, justiciable in this court can be held to exist, something more must be put forward than that the citizens of one State are injured by the maladministration of the laws of another. * * * When there is no agreement, whose breach might create it, a controversy between States does not arise unless the action complained of is state action, and acts of state officers in abuse or excess of their powers cannot be laid hold of as in themselves committing one State to a distinct collision with a sister State."[40]

As the remedies available to independent states were withdrawn from the States of the Union by the Constitution, a wide range of controversies susceptible of adjustment, and not purely political in their nature, was made justiciable by that instrument.[41] But it must be remembered that in controversies between States, it is the *judicial* power that is invoked, and it is a condition of the jurisdiction that the question should be of a sort that admits of a judicial

[39] *Louisiana v. Texas* (1900), 176 U. S. 1; see *Missouri v. Illinois*, 180 U. S. p. 240.

[40] 176 U. S. p. 22.

[41] *Kansas v. Colorado*, 185 U. S. p. 141.

solution.[42] The broad proposal in the Convention that the jurisdiction of the national judiciary should extend to "questions which involve the national peace and harmony"[43] was abandoned in favor of the provisions relating to judicial power and to the cases and controversies in which the judicial power shall be exercised. The line has not yet been drawn definitely between what is justiciable and what is not, but it is clear that there may be serious disputes between States of a political nature with which the judicial power would have no concern.

The State as *parens patriae* may be entitled to invoke the original jurisdiction of the Supreme Court. Missouri brought suit against Illinois for equitable relief against the injury which it was asserted would follow the use of the drainage canal constructed under the authority of Illinois and by the use of which it was alleged the Mississippi river would be polluted and there would be a substantial impairment of the health and prosperity of towns and cities of the State. The Supreme Court took jurisdiction saying that, if the health and comfort of the inhabitants of a State are threatened, the State is the proper party to represent and defend them.[44] Evidence was taken and the case heard on the merits, but as it was found that the evidence failed adequately to support the allegations of the bill

[42] *Louisiana v. Texas*, 176 U. S. p. 18; *Georgia v. Stanton*, 6 Wall. pp. 71-75; *Massachusetts v. Mellon*, 262 U. S. pp. 480, 481.

[43] *Doc. Hist. Const.*, Vol. III, pp. 117, 454, 730.

[44] *Missouri v. Illinois* (1901), 180 U. S. 208.

of complaint, it was dismissed without prejudice.[45]

While this case was pending, Kansas brought suit against Colorado and raised the question whether Colorado had the power to deprive Kansas of the benefit of water from the Arkansas river which rises in Colorado and by nature flows into and through Kansas. Again, the Court took jurisdiction.[46] "Comity," said the Court, "demanded that navigable rivers should be free, and therefore the freedom of the Mississippi, the Rhine, the Scheldt, the Danube, the St. Lawrence, the Amazon, and other rivers has been at different times secured by treaty; but if a State of this Union deprives another State of its rights in a navigable stream, and Congress has not regulated the subject, as no treaty can be made between them, how is the matter to be adjusted?" [47] When the suit came to final hearing,[48] Justice Brewer, speaking for the Court, considered the foundation of the jurisdiction involved. It was said that, speaking generally, "the judicial power of a nation extends to all controversies justiciable in their nature, and the parties to which or the property involved in which may be reached by judicial process, and when the judicial power of the United States was vested in the Supreme and other courts all the judicial power which the Nation was capable of exercising was vested in those tribunals, and unless there

45 *Id.*, (1906) 200 U. S. 496.
46 (1902) 185 U. S. 125.
47 *Id.*, p. 144.
48 (1907) 206 U. S. 46.

be some limitations expressed in the Constitution it must be held to embrace all controversies of a justiciable nature arising within the territorial limits of the Nation, no matter who may be the parties thereto.'' [49] The proposition was laid down that when a legislative power is claimed for the national government the question is whether that power is one of those granted by the Constitution, either in terms or by necessary implication; whereas in respect to judicial functions, the question is whether there be any limitations expressed in the Constitution of the general grant of national power. On the merits, the Court dismissed the bill of Kansas without prejudice to its right to institute new proceedings whenever it should appear that, through a material increase in the depletion of the waters of the Arkansas by Colorado, its corporations or citizens, the substantial interests of Kansas were being injured to the extent of destroying the equitable apportionment between the two States of the benefits resulting from the flow of the river.

About the same time the right of Georgia to bring suit against the Tennessee Copper Company, and to obtain an injunction against the discharging of noxious gases over its territory, was sustained.[50] The Court made further observations with regard to the nature of the suit and the exercise of its jurisdiction, saying: ''This is a suit by a State for an injury to it in its capacity of *quasi*-sovereign. In that capa-

[49] *Id.*, p. 83.
[50] (1907) 206 U. S. 230.

city the State has an interest independent of and be-
hind the titles of its citizens, in all the earth and air
within its domain.  It has the last word as to whether its mountains shall be stripped of their forests
and its inhabitants shall breathe pure air.  It might
have to pay individuals before it could utter that
word, but with it remains the final power.  The alleged damage to the State as a private owner is
merely a make-weight.'' [51] In the case of *New York*
v. *New Jersey* [52] relating to the pollution of New
York Bay by the discharge of sewage from the Pas-
saic Valley, the Court took jurisdiction, saying that
the health, comfort and prosperity of the people of
the State being gravely menaced, as it was averred,
the State was the proper party to defend such rights
by resort to the remedy of an original suit in the Supreme Court.  That suit resulted in a decree denying
the relief asked, without prejudice to the instituting
of another suit for injunction if the operation of the
sewer should prove sufficiently injurious to the waters
of the bay as to lead the State of New York to conclude that the protection of the health, welfare or
commerce of its people required another application.

In *Wyoming* v. *Colorado*,[53] the Court entered a
decree enjoining the defendants from diverting or
taking more than a prescribed amount of water from
the Laramie river by means of a project of which
complaint was made.  In *North Dakota* v. *Minne-*

[51] *Id.*, p. 237.
[52] (1921) 256 U. S. 296.
[53] (1922) 259 U. S. 419.

*sota,*[54] the Court took jurisdiction of a controversy in which Minnesota was charged with having constructed a drainage system by which water was turned into an interstate stream in excess of its capacity so that its banks in North Dakota were flooded to the serious and permanent injury of a valuable area. The Court found on the facts that Minnesota was not responsible for the floods complained of and dismissed the bill without prejudice.

The recent dispute between Pennsylvania and Ohio, on the one side, and West Virginia on the other, as to natural gas showed a serious division of opinion.[55] The Supreme Court, in an opinion by Justice Van Devanter, held that a justiciable controversy was presented. The plaintiff States relied on the commerce clause and sought to enjoin the defendant State from withdrawing natural gas from an established current of commerce moving from her territory into that of the plaintiffs. It was alleged that the withdrawal would cause great injury to the plaintiffs' interests as proprietors of public institutions, and to private consumers, a substantial part of the population, whose health, comfort and welfare would be seriously jeopardized. The Court decided that the action of West Virginia was an unconstitutional interference with interstate commerce and that the appropriate decree was to declare the State act invalid and to enjoin its enforcement. Justices Holmes, McReynolds and Brandeis dissented. Jus-

[54] (1923) 263 U. S. 365.
[55] (1923) 262 U. S. 553, 623; 263 U. S. 350.

tice McReynolds thought the record presented no justiciable controversy. Justice Brandeis thought the Court should not entertain the suit as it would be powerless to frame a decree and provide machinery for an equitable distribution of the available supply of gas. Justice Holmes' dissent went on the merits.

There is now pending in the Supreme Court a suit brought by Wisconsin against Illinois and the Sanitary District of Chicago, in which there are ranged on the side of the plaintiff the States of Minnesota, Michigan, Ohio, Pennsylvania and New York, and, on the side of the defendants, Missouri, Tennessee, Louisiana and Kentucky, with respect to the diversion of the water of Lake Michigan through the Sanitary District Canal at Chicago.

It is manifest that in the exercise of this vastly important jurisdiction over controversies between States, the Supreme Court proceeds with great deliberation. It has not sought to press its authority. "Great States," said Justice Holmes in defining the grounds of liability in *Virginia* v. *West Virginia*,[56] "have a temper superior to that of private litigants, and it is to be hoped that enough has been decided for patriotism, the fraternity of the Union, and mutual consideration to bring it (the suit) to an end." It appeared, however, that enough had not yet been said, but enough to bring about the result was said later. The Supreme Court has emphasized "the untechnical spirit" in which it considers such a case, a spirit "proper for dealing with a quasi-interna-

[56] 220 U. S. p. 36.

tional controversy, remembering that there is no municipal code governing the matter, and that this court may be called on to adjust differences that cannot be dealt with by Congress or disposed of by the legislature of either State alone." [57]

What law does the Supreme Court apply in passing upon such differences? In a boundary dispute, in a suit to recover a debt, or upon a contract, or to prevent an interference with interstate commerce in a recognized subject of that commerce, the principles may be clear, however difficult the application. But what principles are to be invoked to determine other controversies? In *Kansas* v. *Colorado* [58] it was said that, sitting, as it were, as an international, as well as a domestic, tribunal, the Court would apply Federal law, State law, and international law, as the exigencies of the particular case might demand. In *Missouri* v. *Illinois* [59] the Court further elucidated the fundamental questions involved in a suit between States by saying that "if one State raises a controversy with another, this court must determine whether there is any principle of law and, if any, what, on which the plaintiff can recover. But the fact that this court must decide does not mean, of course, that it takes the place of a legislature. Some principles it must have power to declare. * * * But the words of the Constitution would be a narrow ground upon which to construct and apply to the relations between

[57] *Id.*, p. 27.
[58] 185 U. S. pp. 146, 147.
[59] 200 U. S. pp. 519, 520.

States the same system of municipal law in all its details which would be applied between individuals. If we suppose a case which did not fall within the power of Congress to regulate, the result of a declaration of rights by this court would be the establishment of a rule which would be irrevocable by any power except that of this court to reverse its own decision, an amendment of the Constitution, or possibly an agreement between the States sanctioned by the legislature of the United States. The difficulties in the way of establishing such a system of law might not be insuperable, but they would be great and new.'' On the final hearing in *Kansas* v. *Colorado* [60] Justice Brewer made these observations in delivering the opinion of the Court: "One cardinal rule, underlying all the relations of the States to each other, is that of equality of right. Each State stands on the same level with all the rest. It can impose its own legislation on no one of the others, and is bound to yield its own views to none. Yet, whenever, as in the case of *Missouri* v. *Illinois*, * * * the action of one State reaches through the agency of natural laws into the territory of another State, the question of the extent and the limitations of the rights of the two States becomes a matter of justiciable dispute between them, and this court is called upon to settle that dispute in such a way as will recognize the equal rights of both and at the same time establish justice between them. In other words, through these successive disputes and decisions this

[60] 206 U. S. pp. 97, 98.

court is practically building up what may not improperly be called interstate common law.''

But little progress has been made in the development of this system of law. This department of jurisprudence is in the making. With the settlement of boundary disputes new questions are coming to the front, and it is believed that the jurisdiction of the Supreme Court to determine controversies between the States will be of increasing importance. This is an era of the development and use of hydro-electric power and thus a new field of controversy between the States has been opened.

The case of *Kansas* v. *Colorado* gave opportunity for the Supreme Court to consider the doctrine of ''sovereign and inherent power'' in the national government, a doctrine advanced on an application by the United States to intervene in the controversy because the national government claimed the right broadly to legislate for the reclamation of arid lands and to appropriate the accessible waters for this purpose. The argument for the Government was, in substance: ''All legislative power must be vested in either the state or the National Government; no legislative powers belong to a state government other than those which affect solely the internal affairs of that State; consequently all powers which are national in their scope must be found vested in the Congress of the United States.'' [61] The Court denied the contention, pointing out that the reclamation of arid lands, not the property of the United

[61] *Id.*, p. 89.

States nor situated within the limits of a territory, was not comprehended in the grant to Congress of the power to dispose of, and control and regulate, the territory or other property of the United States. It gave no legislative control over the States, and must so far as they are concerned be limited to property of the United States within their limits. The Court said that the argument for the Government ignored the provisions of the Tenth Amendment, the principal purpose of which was not a distribution of power between the United States and the States, but a reservation to the people of all the powers not granted. "The powers affecting the internal affairs of the States not granted to the United States by the Constitution, nor prohibited by it to the States, are reserved to the States respectively, and all powers of a national character which are not delegated to the National Government by the Constitution are reserved to the people of the United States." [62] The question, it will be noted, was not of the authority of Congress to take whatever measures may be necessary in the execution of its granted powers, but of supposed sovereign or inherent powers in addition to those found in the terms of the grant. Accordingly, the petition of the United States to intervene was dismissed without prejudice to the rights of the United States to take such action as it shall deem necessary to preserve or improve the navigability of the Arkansas river.

While the system of what may be called interstate

[62] *Id.*, p. 90.

law, relating to the rights and obligations of the States *inter sese,* not defined by the Constitution, waits on the future, the principles governing the regulation of commerce among the several States and with foreign nations, are well established. Recognizing the necessity for confiding the power of regulation to the Federal Government, and to its legislative department, and that the Constitution owes its very existence to the economic exigency arising from the lack of unified control of commerce, we may still marvel at the willingness of the framers to make this grant in such general terms and without the qualifications upon which it would seem natural for the States to have insisted. Chief Justice Marshall referred to the oppressed and degraded state of commerce previous to the adoption of the Constitution. "It was regulated by foreign nations with a single view to their own interests; and our disunited efforts to counteract their restrictions were rendered impotent by want of combination." "It may be doubted," said he, "whether any of the evils proceeding from the feebleness of the federal government, contributed more to that great revolution which introduced the present system, than the deep and general conviction, that commerce ought to be regulated by Congress." "It is not, therefore, matter of surprise, that the grant should be as extensive as the mischief, and should comprehend all foreign commerce, and all commerce among the States." [63] In no respect has the wisdom of the founders been

[63] *Brown v. Maryland* (1827), 12 Wheaton, pp. 445, 446.

more completely justified. In the case of *Debs* [64] Justice Brewer remarked that constitutional provisions do not change, but their operation extends to new matters as the modes of business and the habits of life vary with each succeeding generation. The power is the same. The extraordinary thing is not that the power does not change, but that in the era of railroads, telegraphs, telephones, wireless communication and distribution of electric power, the authority granted in the days of the coach and wagon, the sailing vessel and canal boat, should be adequate to the most varied commercial activities on the largest scale of freedom of communications and exchanges that the world has ever known. The commerce clause has not been enlarged; it has simply been applied. The fact that the grant was broad and was closely related to the needs of a developing country has given to the Supreme Court its weightiest responsibility and affords the clearest vindication of the exercise of its distinctive function. It was necessary that the sound judgment of the Court should match the wisdom of the fathers in order to make such a scheme work satisfactorily.

It was many years before Congress exercised its power over interstate commerce to any important extent. During the first fifty years, only five cases involving the construction of the commerce clause were brought before the Supreme Court; and up to 1870, the number of such cases was only thirty. Since then, the number has increased rapidly, and

[64] (1895) 158 U. S. 564, 591.

Federal legislation under this power has become the most significant feature of the legislative history of our time. Although the decisions in the early period were few, we go back one hundred and twelve years to find the announcement of the principle which has been the guiding star of the Court. Nothing is more striking in our constitutional jurisprudence than the extent to which fundamental principles were early determined. It is true that the questions of due process and equal protection in relation to State action have arisen in recent years out of the Fourteenth Amendment. But the doctrine of implied powers, of the wide scope of national authority in executing the enumerated powers, was laid down by Marshall in 1819 in the *Mc-Culloch* case,[65] and it is in accordance with the exposition by the great Chief Justice in *Gibbons* v. *Ogden* [66] in 1824 that the Supreme Court applies the commerce clause in the twentieth century. We go back to Marshall for the best definition of commerce. "Commerce," said he, "undoubtedly, is traffic, but it is something more: it is intercourse. It describes the commercial intercourse between nations, and parts of nations, in all its branches." [67] It is to Marshall that we turn for the description of the power confided to Congress and its scope. "What is this

[65] 4 Wheaton, 316.

[66] 9 Wheaton, 1.

[67] *Id.*, pp. 189, 190. But the Supreme Court adheres to the view that insurance is not commerce, *Paul v. Virginia*, (1869) 8 Wallace, 168; *New York Life Ins. Co. v. Deer Lodge County* (1913), 231 U. S. 495.

power? It is the power to regulate; that is, to prescribe the rule by which commerce is to be governed. This power, like all others vested in Congress, is complete in itself, may be exercised to its utmost extent, and acknowledges no limitations, other than are prescribed in the constitution."[68] Again, as to the supremacy of the power of Congress, he said: "If, as has always been understood, the sovereignty of Congress, though limited to specified objects, is plenary as to those objects, the power over commerce with foreign nations, and among the several States, is vested in Congress as absolutely as it would be in a single government, having in its constitution the same restrictions on the exercise of the power as are found in the constitution of the United States. * * * Powerful and ingenious minds, taking, as postulates, that the powers expressly granted to the government of the Union, are to be contracted by construction, into the narrowest possible compass, and that the original powers of the States are retained, if any possible construction will retain them, may, by a course of well digested, but refined and metaphysical reasoning, founded on these premises, explain away the constitution of our country, and leave it, a magnificent structure, indeed, to look at, but totally unfit for use. They may so entangle and perplex the understanding, as to obscure principles, which were before thought quite plain, and induce doubts where, if the mind were to pursue its own course, none would be perceived. In such a

[68] *Id.*, p. 196.

case, it is peculiarly necessary to recur to safe and fundamental principles to sustain those principles, and, when sustained, to make them the tests of the arguments to be examined.'' [69]

It would be impossible for me in this course of lectures to state, much less to attempt to appraise, the numerous decisions of the Supreme Court on this subject. Almost every one of them has been attended by keen controversy, by a conflict in the views of the ablest men of the time, and by the arguments of eminent counsel in opposition to the opinion finally dominant; not infrequently, the views of the Court have been challenged by the sharp dissent of some of its members. The course of decisions has not been free from inconsistencies. Yet, whatever may be said of this or that decision in particular, out of all the debate and criticism has come a general acquiescence, I believe, in the established doctrines of the Court. In considering the general results of the work of the Court in this field, a distinction may be taken between what may be called the negative effects of the commerce clause and affirmative action taken by Congress under it. The commerce clause itself, without action by Congress, is a charter of freedom in interstate and foreign commerce from State interference with respect to those activities which in view of their nature demand uniformity of regulation, if they are to be regulated at all. In such matters, the silence of Congress indicates that this freedom is to be left unimpaired. It is in this

[69] *Id.*, pp. 197, 222.

sense that it has been held that the States cannot impose what is deemed to be a ''direct burden'' on interstate commerce.[70] Thus, the States cannot tax interstate commerce, either by laying the tax upon the business which constitutes such commerce or upon the privilege of engaging in it, or upon the receipts, as such, derived from it, or upon persons or property in transit in interstate commerce. The States have no power to prohibit interstate trade in legitimate articles of commerce, or to discriminate against the products of other States, or to exclude from the limits of the State, corporations or others engaged in interstate commerce, or to fetter by conditions their right to carry it on. The States cannot prescribe the rates to be charged for transportation from one State to another, or subject the operations of carriers in the course of such transportation to requirements that are unreasonable or that pass beyond the bounds of suitable local protection. A short time ago the Supreme Court in an opinion by Justice Sanford decided that a State cannot regulate the rates charged by a local electrical corporation for current sold to a corporation of an adjoining State for use in that State and delivered at the State boundary.[71] At the same time, it was ruled that the soliciting of passengers and the sale of steamship tickets and orders for passage between the United States and Europe constitute a part of

[70] *Minnesota Rate Cases* (1913), 230 U. S. pp. 400-402.

[71] *Public Utilities Commission v. Attleboro Steam & Electric Co.* (1927), 273 U. S. 83.

foreign commerce with which the State could not interfere by requiring licenses to engage in it. The
statute, said Justice Butler in delivering the opinion, was a "direct burden" on that commerce.[72]

It is plain, however, that if the States, in the absence of any conflicting congressional action, were
denied the right to prescribe any rules which might
affect interstate or foreign commerce, their interests
would be seriously impaired. The States have vast
internal commerce which is their special concern.
Their legislation for the purpose of protecting that
commerce, where it does not impinge on Federal action within the Federal sphere, is necessary. In the
intimacy of commercial relations much that is done
in the superintendence of local matters may have an
indirect bearing on interstate commerce. The development of local resources, and the extension of local
facilities, may have a very important effect upon
communities less favored and to an appreciable degree may alter the course of trade. The freedom of
local trade may stimulate interstate commerce while
restrictive measures within the police power of the
State, enacted exclusively with respect to internal
business, may in their reflex influence reduce the
volume of articles transported into or out of the
States. Aside from such action, the power of the
States may also extend to interstate and foreign
commerce where the matter, although directly relating to such commerce, has an essentially local aspect.
Thus, there necessarily remains to the States, until

[72] *Di Santo v. Pennsylvania* (1927), 273 U. S. 34.

Congress acts under its authority, a wide range for the permissible exercise of power appropriate to their territorial jurisdiction. From the foundation of the Government, certain subjects having the most obvious and direct relation to interstate and foreign commerce have, with the acquiescence of Congress, been controlled by State legislation, because of the necessity that they should not go unregulated and that their regulation should be adapted to varying local exigencies. Our system of government is a practical adjustment by which the national authority as conferred by the Constitution is maintained in its full scope without unnecessary loss of local efficiency. Illustrations of the State power, to which I have just referred, are found in the cases of pilotage, local improvements of navigable streams and harbors, regulation of wharfage charges and tolls for the use of artificial facilities provided by the State, quarantine regulations for the protection of health, and inspection laws and other measures to safeguard against fraud and imposition. Congress must be the judge of the necessity of Federal action within its competency, and its paramount power always enables it to intervene at its discretion for the complete and effective government of that which has been committed to its care, and for this purpose and to this extent in response to a conviction of national need, to displace local regulations by substituting laws of its own.[73]

This important principle, governing the decision

[73] *Minnesota Rate Cases,* 230 U. S. pp. 402-412.

of controversies as to the field within which the State
power can be exercised in the absence of congressional action, was established by the Supreme Court
in 1851 in the case of *Cooley* v. *Port Wardens*,[74] relating to pilotage, Justice Curtis writing the opinion.   His summary which gave the formula for solving some of the most difficult problems that have come
before the Court is as follows:   "Now the power to
regulate commerce, embraces a vast field, containing
not only many, but exceedingly various subjects,
quite unlike in their nature; some imperatively demanding a single uniform rule, operating equally on
the commerce of the United States in every port; and
some, like the subject now in question, as imperatively demanding that diversity, which alone can meet
the local necessities of navigation.   Either absolutely to affirm, or deny that the nature of this power
requires exclusive legislation by Congress, is to lose
sight of the nature of the subjects of this power, and
to assert concerning all of them, what is really applicable but to a part.   Whatever subjects of this
power are in their nature national, or admit only of
one uniform system, or plan of regulation, may just-
ly be said to be of such a nature as to require exclusive legislation by Congress."   That could not be
said of laws for the regulation of pilotage and from
the beginning that subject had been left to State
legislation.   "How, then, can we say," continued
Justice Curtis, "that by the mere grant of power to
regulate commerce, the States are deprived of all

[74] 12 Howard, 299.

the power to legislate on this subject, because from the nature of the power the legislation of Congress must be exclusive.  This would be to affirm that the nature of the power is in any case, something different from the nature of the subject to which, in such case, the power extends, and that the nature of the power necessarily demands, in all cases, exclusive legislation by Congress, while the nature of one of the subjects of that power, not only does not require such exclusive legislation, but may be best provided for by many different systems enacted by the States, in conformity with the circumstances of the ports within their limits.'' [75]

When Congress acts competently, conflicting State legislation of any sort must yield.  It was upon this ground that Chief Justice Marshall rested the decision of *Gibbons* v. *Ogden*,[76] that is, that the legislative acts of New York, giving to Robert R. Livingston and Robert Fulton exclusive navigation of all the waters within the jurisdiction of that State with boats moved by fire or steam, were in collision with the Acts of Congress regulating the coasting trade. A corollary of this proposition is that if Congress by its action has taken possession of a particular field, State action in the same field is negatived although Congress may not have dealt with the precise point. Thus, the Supreme Court decided that Congress had so acted on the subject of hours of labor of interstate railway employees by the Act of 1907[77] as to preclude

[75] *Id.*, pp. 319, 320.
[76] 9 Wheaton, 1.
[77] 34 Statutes at Large, 1415.

the State during the period between the date of that Act and the time that it went into effect from making a regulation affecting the hours of such employees. As the authority of the State to deal with the matter existed only by virtue of the willingness of Congress, that authority ceased when Congress manifested its purpose "to call into play its exclusive power."[78] But Congress in dealing with a subject within its power may see fit to circumscribe its regulation and to occupy a limited field so that the State may still be able to care for its local needs without proceeding contrary to the congressional action.[79] The question is, — Does the action of Congress, fairly interpreted, conflict with the law of the State? These general principles established by the Supreme Court in construing the commerce clause show the highest level of judicial wisdom and statesmanship. The difficulty constantly apparent in the great variety of cases brought before the Court lies not in present disagreement with respect to these principles but in applying them.

I have spoken of the negative effect of the Constitution, and of the laws under its authority, that is, their effect in overriding State legislation. How far does the power of Congress go in its affirmative action under the commerce clause. The power to regulate is the power "to foster, protect, control and restrain."[80] Chief Justice Marshall said that it was

[78] *Northern Pacific Railway Co. v. Washington* (1912), 222 U. S. 370, 378.

[79] *Savage v. Jones* (1912), 225 U. S. 501.

[80] *Second Employers' Liability Cases* (1912), 223 U. S. 1, 47.

as wide as the exigencies which called it into existence, and it may be added that under the decisions
of the Supreme Court it remains as wide as the
modern exigencies it must meet in relation to interstate and foreign commerce.  Few lawyers, forty
years ago, would have dreamed of the extensive
schemes of Federal legislation which have successfully passed judicial scrutiny as to their constitutional validity.   In rapid succession we have had the
Interstate Commerce Act, with the Hepburn and
Carmack Amendments and those of the Transportation Act, 1920; the Anti-Trust Acts; the Safety Ap-
pliance Act; the Hours of Service Act; the Employers' Liability Act; the Adamson Act; the Pure Food
and Drugs Act; the Meat Inspection Act; the White
Slave Traffic Act; the Harrison Narcotic Act; and
many others.   In the opinion sustaining the second
Employers' Liability Act,[81] which abrogated the fel-
low-servant rule and restricted the defenses of con-
tributory negligence and assumption of risk (relating to the employees, engaged in interstate commerce, of interstate carriers), Justice Van Devanter
pointed out that the action of Congress would super-
sede the State action which previously had been appropriate and had been taken with respect to subjects falling within the police power of the States.
Congress established its own measure of liability,
and the State courts, as well as the Federal courts,
must recognize it.   Congress thereby established a
policy for all, and that policy became as much the

[81] *Id.*, pp. 55, 57.

policy of the States as if the act had emanated from their own legislatures.

There are three outstanding characteristics of the recent legislation of Congress under the commerce clause.  One is, not simply the broad action of Congress in relation to transactions in interstate commerce, but the entry of Congress, either directly or through its agencies, into what many had supposed to be the exclusive province of the State in dealing with intrastate activities.  This has not been due to the recognition of any power of Congress to deal with the internal concerns of the State, as such, but to the commingling of interstate and intrastate transactions, so that the government of the one involves to an extent the government of the other. In the case of railroads, the same right of way, terminals, rails, bridges and stations are used for both interstate and local traffic.  Terminals, facilities, and connections in one State aid the carrier's entire business; securities are issued against the entire line without reference to what are interstate or intrastate transactions.  It thus had to be recognized that wherever the interstate and intrastate activities were so interwoven that the regulation of the one involved the control of the other, it is Congress and not the State that is entitled to prescribe the final and dominant rule, for otherwise Congress would be denied the exercise of its constitutional authority, and the State, and not the Nation, would be supreme within the national field.  Thus, in order to avoid discrimination against interstate traffic, it has been necessary for the Interstate Commerce Commission acting under the authority of Congress, to prescribe rules governing intrastate transportation.[82]

Another characteristic is the extension of the authority of administrative bodies equipped with power to determine questions of fact beyond judicial review, providing action is taken within the authority properly delegated and the essentials of due process are observed. Evils must be controlled and the exercise of legislative power must be broad enough to cope with the difficulty of solving the many questions of fact in a host of particular instances which lie within the sphere of the application of legislative standards. To an increasing degree the activities of commerce are falling into the control of bureaus and commissions.

The third characteristic is that Congress in establishing its regulations is exercising authority closely akin to the police power. The Supreme Court has frequently said that the United States lacks the police power, and that this was reserved to the States by the Tenth Amendment.[83] What is meant by this? That the Federal Government has no general governmental authority outside the powers granted to it. "But it is none the less true that when the United States exerts any of the powers conferred upon it by the Constitution, no valid objection can be based upon the fact that such exercise

[82] *The Shreveport Case* (1914), 234 U. S. 342; *Wisconsin Railroad Commission v. Chicago, B. & Q. R. R. Co.* (1922), 257 U. S. 563.

[83] *Hamilton v. Kentucky Distilleries Co.* (1919), 251 U. S. 146, 156.

may be attended by the same incidents which attend the exercise by a State of its police power, or that it may tend to accomplish a similar purpose."[84] What is the police power of the State? It is the power to care for the health, safety, morals and welfare of the people. In a general way, it extends to all the great public needs.[85] It is subject in its exercise to limitations of both the State and the Federal constitutions. It is a fallacy to suppose that it cannot be overridden by Federal power. It is overridden whenever Federal power is exercised within its constitutional limits with respect to any conflicting State action. The question, when the Federal Government acts, is whether it acts within the limited powers conferred. Because Congress was found to be acting within its authority over interstate commerce, the Supreme Court sustained, for example, the interdiction of the carriage from one State to another of lottery tickets,[86] of impure foods,[87] of diseased animals,[88] of women for purposes of prostitution.[89] Acting within the scope of its war power Congress established wartime prohibition.[90] These measures were found none the less to be within the authority of Congress because they had the quality of police regulations.

The distinction to be observed is between the ex-

[84] *Id.*

[85] *Noble State Bank v. Haskell* (1911), 219 U. S. 104, 111.

[86] *Lottery Case* (1903), 188 U. S. 321, 357.

[87] *Hipolite Egg Co. v. United States* (1911), 220 U. S. 45, 58.

[88] *Reid v. Colorado* (1902), 187 U. S. 137.

[89] *Hoke v. United States* (1913), 227 U. S. 308, 322.

[90] *Hamilton v. Kentucky Distilleries Co.* (1919), 251 U. S. 146.

ercise of the power of Congress over a subject committed to it and its attempt to establish a regulation over a subject not committed to it.   The most striking illustration of the difficulty in maintaining this distinction is in the first child labor case,[91] to which I have already alluded.   Congress had undertaken to prohibit the transportation in interstate commerce of goods made in a factory in which, within thirty days prior to the removal of the goods, children of a certain age had been employed.   It was found that the goods in question were of themselves entirely harmless; their production in the factory was not commerce, and the power of Congress did not extend to that production.   It was decided, against strong dissent, that Congress was endeavoring to control production within the State under the guise of regulating commerce among the States.   Justice Day, in giving the opinion of the Court,[92] indicated the far-reaching result of a contrary view by pointing out that if Congress could thus regulate matters entrusted to local authority, by the prohibition of the movement of articles in interstate commerce, the power of the States over local matters would be eliminated and our system of government would practically be destroyed.

[91] *Hammer v. Dagenhart* (1918), 247 U. S. 251.
[92] *Id.*, p. 276.

## V

## Liberty, Property and Social Justice

Jefferson, who was in Paris when the Federal Convention was at work, wrote to Madison in December, 1787, expressing general approval of the Constitution but strongly criticizing the absence of a bill of rights. He desired such a declaration "providing clearly & without the aid of sophisms for freedom of religion, freedom of the press, protection against standing armies, restriction against monopolies, the eternal & unremitting force of the habeas corpus laws, and trials by jury in all matters of fact triable by the laws of the land & not by the law of Nations." [1] He wished "to guard liberty against the legislative as well as executive branches of the government." [2] No effort had been made in the Convention to incorporate a bill of rights until the session was nearly over and then the proposal was defeated. It was believed to be unnecessary. Hamilton, in the Federalist,[3] pointed to the provisions as to impeachment, *habeas corpus*, bills of attainder and *ex post facto* laws, prohibition of titles of nobility, trial by jury in cases of crime, and treason.

[1] *Doct. Hist. Const.*, Vol. IV, p. 412.
[2] Letter to F. Hopkinson, March 13, 1789, *id.*, Vol. V, p. 159.
[3] No. LXXXIV.

He urged that the inclusion of a bill of rights in the sense contended for would be dangerous as containing exceptions to powers not granted, and they would afford a colorable pretext to claim more than were granted. "For why declare that things shall not be done which there is no power to do?" [4] But the popular insistence for a bill of rights was too strong to be ignored. Serious fears were entertained that the powers deemed to be essential to the Union might be exercised in a manner dangerous to liberty and in almost every Convention by which the Constitution was adopted amendments to guard against the abuse of power were recommended. The first Congress under the Constitution made response to this widespread demand by submitting twelve amendments, of which ten were ratified. These amendments covered freedom of religion, of speech, of the press, and the right of petition; the right of the people to bear arms is not to be infringed; abuses through the quartering of troops are controlled; unreasonable searches and seizures are forbidden; trial for a capital or otherwise infamous crime must be on presentment or indictment of the grand jury, except in the army and navy or in the militia when in actual service; there must not be double jeopardy; witnesses are protected against compulsory self-incrimination; no person is to be deprived of life, liberty or property without due process of law; private property is not to be taken for public use without

[4] *Id.*

just compensation; protection to the accused in criminal prosecutions is provided by requiring speedy and public trial by an impartial jury of the State and district where the crime was committed, confrontation of witnesses, the privilege of compulsory process for obtaining witnesses and the assistance of counsel for defense; trial by jury is preserved in civil actions; excessive bail, excessive fines and cruel and unusual punishments are prohibited; the enumeration of certain rights in the Constitution is not to be construed to deny or disparage others retained by the people; and the powers not delegated to the United States, nor prohibited to the States, are reserved to the States respectively, or to the people.

These ten amendments have no application to the State governments; they apply to the Federal government alone.[5] The Constitution prohibited the States from passing bills of attainder, *ex post facto* laws, or laws impairing the obligations of contracts,[6] but it was not until the adoption of the Fourteenth Amendment, in 1868, that State action was subjected to the "due process" and "equal protection" clauses. The muniments of liberty and property contained in the first ten amendments were undoubtedly intended to give protection against Congress as well as against the executive branch of the government. The maintenance of this protection as against both legislative and executive action rests with the courts,

[5] *Barron v. Baltimore* (1833), 7 Peters, 243, 250.
[6] Art. I, Sec. 10.

and especially with the Supreme Court, as the repository of the judicial power. This was distinctly stated by Madison who was the leading spirit in the preparation of the amendments. Said he: "If they are incorporated into the Constitution, independent tribunals of justice will consider themselves in a peculiar manner the guardians of those rights; they will be an impenetrable bulwark against every assumption of power in the Legislative or Executive; they will be naturally led to resist every encroachment upon rights expressly stipulated for in the Constitution by the declaration of rights." [7]

How far has this expectation been realized with respect to the essentials of liberty? A few illustrations may be given. Freedom of religion, of speech and of the press, are among the first of these essentials. "Religion" is not defined in the Constitution and it is necessary to recur to the history of the times in which the provision was adopted. Attempts had been made in some of the Colonies and States to legislate not only in respect to the establishment of religion, but as to its doctrines and precepts as well. The people were taxed against their will for the support of religion, and sometimes for the support of particular sects to whose tenets they did not subscribe. There were punishments for a failure to attend public worship, and sometimes for heretical opinions. [8] The oppressive measures which

[7] *Annals of Congress*, Vol. I, 1st Cong., 1st and 2d Sess., p. 439.

[8] *Reynolds v. United States* (1879), 98 U. S. 145, 162, 163; *Davis v. Beason* (1890), 133 U. S. 333, 342.

had been adopted, and the cruelties and punishments which had been inflicted, by the governments of Europe to compel conformity in religious beliefs and modes of worship to the views of the most numerous sect, and the folly of attempting in that way to control the mental operations of persons, and enforce an outward compliance with a prescribed standard, led to the adoption of the First Amendment. "It was under a solemn consciousness," to use the words of Story, "of the dangers from ecclesiastical ambition, the bigotry of spiritual pride, and the intolerance of sects, thus exemplified in our domestic as well as in foreign annals, that it was deemed advisable to exclude from the national government all power to act upon the subject." [9] This Amendment providing "that Congress shall make no law respecting an establishment of religion, or prohibiting the free exercise thereof" was proposed by Madison and met the views of the advocates of religious freedom. In reviewing these facts, Chief Justice Waite delivering the opinion of the Supreme Court in *Reynolds* v. *United States* quoted the following reply by Jefferson to an address to him by a committee of the Danbury Baptist Association: "Believing with you that religion is a matter which lies solely between man and his God; that he owes account to none other for his faith or his worship; that the legislative powers of the government reach actions only, and not opinions, — I contemplate with sovereign reverence that

[9] *Story on the Constitution*, Vol. II, Sec. 1879.

act of the whole American people which declared
that their legislature should 'make no law respecting
an establishment of religion or prohibiting the free
exercise thereof,' thus building a wall of separation
between church and State. Adhering to this expression of the supreme will of the nation in behalf of
the rights of conscience, I shall see with sincere satisfaction the progress of those sentiments which
tend to restore man to all his natural rights, convinced he has no natural right in opposition to his
social duties.'' [10] Chief Justice Waite said that this
statement coming from an acknowledged leader of
the advocates of the measure ''may be accepted almost as an authoritative declaration of the scope and
effect of the amendment.'' The established principle
was thus declared by the Supreme Court to be:
''Congress was deprived of all legislative power
over mere opinion, but was left free to reach actions
which were in violation of social duties or subversive
of good order.'' [11] Applying this principle, the Supreme Court held that the guaranteed freedom of
religion did not constitute a justification of polyg-
amy which had been made criminal by an act of Congress applicable to the territories.[12] The First
Amendment could not be invoked as a protection
against legislation for the punishment of acts inimical to the good order and morals of society. It is the

[10] (1879), 98 U. S. p. 164.
[11] *Id.*
[12] *Id., Davis v. Beason* (1890), 133 U. S. 333.

function of the Supreme Court to maintain this balance between the constitutional guarantees of liberty and legislative requirements in the interest of the social order.

By reason of our happy tradition, there was little occasion prior to the Great War to deal with violations of the First Amendment with respect to the liberty of the press and of speech. The Sedition Law of 1798 [13] which aroused such violent antagonism expired by its own limitation in 1801 and did not come before the Supreme Court. The historical background of the provision as to freedom of the press is familiar. The art of printing had been looked upon in England, as in other countries, as a matter of State and subject to the coercion of the Crown. It had been regulated in England by the King's proclamations, by prohibitions, charters of privilege and licenses. The Long Parliament assumed the same powers as those which had been exercised by the Star Chamber with respect to licensing books and during the Commonwealth ordinances were issued for that purpose founded principally upon a Star Chamber decree. A similar statute was passed after the Restoration, but because of the resistance of Parliament was permitted to expire in 1694 and was not revived.[14] In other countries, the press had been shackled and "compelled to speak only in the timid language which the cringing courtier or the caprici-

[13] 1 Statutes at Large, 596.
[14] *Story on the Constitution*, Vol. II, Sec. 1882.

ous inquisitor, should license for publication." [15]
"The main purpose of such constitutional provisions," it has been said, "is 'to prevent all such *previous restraints* upon publications as had been practiced by other governments,' and they do not prevent the subsequent punishment of such as may be deemed contrary to the public welfare." [16] Libel and attempts to disturb the public peace and to subvert the government are left subject to appropriate penalties. It is obvious, however, that if the freedom of the press meant no more than immunity from restraint in advance of publication, and if the legislative power extended without restriction to the punishment of the publication after it had been made, the immunity would be of little value. The tests to be applied to freedom both of the press and of speech were laid down by the Supreme Court in the cases arising under the Espionage Act of 1917.[17] There were four of these cases in which the decisions of the Court were unanimous.[18] It was recognized that the constitutional prohibition was not confined to previous restraint of publication, although that might have been its main purpose. The question in every case was whether the words were used in such circumstances and were of such a nature as to create

[15] *Id.*, Sec. 1881.

[16] *Patterson v. Colorado* (1907), 205 U. S. 454, 462.

[17] 40 Statutes at Large, 217, 219.

[18] *Schenck v. United States* (1919), 249 U. S. 47; *Sugarman v. United States* (1919), 249 U. S. 182; *Frohwerk v. United States* (1919), 249 U. S. 204; *Debs. v. United States* (1919), 249 U. S. 211.

"a clear and present danger" that they will bring about the substantive evils that Congress had the right to prevent. It is a question of "proximity and degree." When a nation is at war many things that might be said in time of peace are such a hindrance to its effort that their utterance cannot be endured and no court could regard them as protected by any constitutional right.[19] "The most stringent protection of free speech," said Justice Holmes, "would not protect a man in falsely shouting fire in a theater, and causing a panic. It does not even protect a man from an injunction against uttering words that may have all the effect of force." Liability for words that had the consequence of causing an actual obstruction of the recruiting service could be enforced. So, if the act, (speaking, or circulating a paper) its tendency and the intent with which it is done, are the same, there would be no ground for saying that success alone warrants making the act a crime.[20] In later cases,[21] there was a sharp division in the Court, but this apparently was with respect to the application of these principles to particular facts rather than as to the principles themselves. The division in the Court illustrates the vast importance of its function, as, after all, the protection both of the rights of the in-

[19] *Schenck v. United States*, 249 U. S. p. 52.

[20] *Id.*

[21] *Abrams v. United States* (1919), 250 U. S. 616; *Schaefer v. United States* (1920), 251 U. S. 466; *Pierce v. United States* (1920), 252 U. S. 239.

dividual and of those of society rests not so often on formulas, as to which there may be agreement, but on a correct appreciation of social conditions and a true appraisal of the actual effect of conduct.

In order to make it unnecessary to recur to the subject, I may say at this point that it was once remarked in an opinion of the Supreme Court that the Constitution did not impose on the States any obligation to maintain the right of free speech.[22] But this remark has been withdrawn and in the *Gitlow* case [23] reviewing a conviction under the laws of the State of New York, the Court assumed that freedom of speech and of the press, protected by the First Amendment from abridgment by Congress, is among the fundamental personal rights and liberties protected by the due process clause of the Fourteenth Amendment from impairment by the States. On this assumption, it was decided that a State in the exercise of its police power may punish those who abuse this freedom "by utterances inimical to the public welfare, tending to corrupt public morals, incite to crime, or disturb the public peace." [24] The statute which was upheld in that case penalized utterances advocating the overthrow of organized government by force, violence or any unlawful means. The question was considered in the light of the principle that the State was primarily the judge of regulations re-

[22] *Prudential Insurance Co. v. Cheek* (1922), 259 U. S. 530, 538.
[23] *Gitlow v. New York* (1925), 268 U. S. 652, 666.
[24] *Id.*, p. 667.

quired for the protection of the public, and that its police statutes could be declared unconstitutional only if they were of an arbitrary character. The minority did not disagree with the opinion of the Court as to the scope of the Fourteenth Amendment, but thought that the test should be that laid down by the full court under the Federal Espionage Act to which I have alluded.[25]

The question as to the extent of the freedom of the press also arises in proceedings for contempt of court. Many years ago Congress passed an act providing that the Federal courts should have authority to punish for contempt by fine or imprisonment, at the discretion of the court, when the misbehavior was in their presence or so near thereto as to obstruct the administration of justice.[26] A Toledo newspaper, while a suit was pending in the Federal court involving the validity of a municipal ordinance relat-

[25] *Id.*, pp. 670, 671, 672, 673. Since this lecture was delivered, the Supreme Court has followed the *Gitlow* case in *Whitney v. California* (May 16, 1927) sustaining the Criminal Syndicalism Act of that State. It was held that the statute was not an arbitrary exercise of the police power of the State, as the ''essence of the offense denounced by the Act is the combination with others in an association for the accomplishment of the desired ends through the advocacy and use of criminal and unlawful methods.'' While Justices Brandeis and Holmes concurred in the result because the errors alleged were not properly before the Court, they dissented from the reasoning of the Court's opinion. They urged that ''the necessity which is essential to a valid restriction does not exist unless speech would produce, or is intended to produce, a clear and imminent danger of some substantive evil which the State constitutionally may seek to prevent.''

[26] 4 Statutes at Large, 487.

ing to street railway fares, challenged the right of the court to grant relief and made its proceedings the subject of extreme criticism. Proceedings were instituted to punish for contempt and the newspaper's comments on this action were then charged to be a further contempt. The case came before the Supreme Court to determine the power of the court below to inflict punishment.[27] Chief Justice White delivering the opinion observed that the "safeguarding and fructification of free and constitutional institutions is the very basis and mainstay on which the freedom of the press rests, and that freedom, therefore, does not and cannot be held to include the right virtually to destroy such institutions." It appeared from the findings, which were considered to be adequately supported by the evidence, that the publications tended, and were intended, to provoke public resistance to an injunction order and constituted an attempt to intimidate — at least unduly to influence — the District Judge. In this view, the right to punish was sustained.[28] The situation with which the trial court had to deal was said to be controlled by "the reasonable tendencies of the acts done" and not by extreme assumptions. Justice Holmes, with whom Justice Brandeis concurred in dissent, thought that the provision of the statute as to misbehavior "in their presence, or so near thereto as to obstruct the administration of justice" meant

[27] *Toledo Newspaper Co. v. United States* (1918), 247 U. S. 402.
[28] *Id.*, pp. 419-421.

"so near as actually to obstruct — and not merely near enough to threaten a possible obstruction." Assuming an imminent possibility of obstruction to be sufficient, he thought that there was no emergency in the instant case. He said: "I would go as far as any man in favor of the sharpest and most summary enforcement of order in court and obedience to decrees, but when there is no need for immediate action, contempts are like any other breach of law and should be dealt with as the law deals with other illegal acts." [29] It will be observed that the division in the Court apparently rested on the effect of what had been done and said rather than on the appropriate rule of law to be applied.

The Fourth Amendment, safeguarding against unreasonable searches and seizures, was interpreted in the opinion of Justice Bradley in the case of *Boyd* v. *United States*.[30] It was decided that it did not require an actual entry upon premises, and search for and seizure of property, to violate this amendment, but that a compulsory production of a party's private books and papers to be used against himself or his property in a criminal, or penal proceeding or for a forfeiture, was within the spirit and meaning of the constitutional provision. "Papers," said the court, quoting from Lord Camden, "are the owner's goods and chattels; they are his dearest property." It was in this opinion that Justice Bradley sounded

[29] *Id.*, pp. 423-426.
[30] (1886), 116 U. S. 616.

his eloquent warning against permitting invasions of constitutional rights because they were of a relatively mild and but slightly offensive character; "illegitimate and unconstitutional practices get their first footing in that way, namely: by silent approaches and slight deviations from legal modes of procedure. This can only be obviated by adhering to the rule that constitutional provisions for the security of person and property should be liberally construed. A close and literal construction deprives them of half of their efficacy and leads to gradual depreciation of the right, as if it consisted more in sound than in substance. It is the duty of the courts to be watchful for the constitutional rights of the citizen, and against any stealthy encroachments thereon. Their motto should be *obsta principiis*." [31] Down to the adoption of the Eighteenth Amendment, and the passage of the Volstead Act, there was comparatively little occasion for the Supreme Court to construe the Fourth Amendment. The new policy has raised many questions. There was elaborate examination of some of these in a recent opinion of Chief Justice Taft.[32] The Chief Justice said that the Fourth Amendment "is to be construed in the light of what was deemed an unreasonable search and seizure when it was adopted, and in a manner which will conserve public interests as well as the interests and rights of individual citizens." After an extended

[31] *Id.*, pp. 627, 635.
[32] *Carroll v. United States* (1925), 267 U. S. 132.

review of legislation, the conclusion was reached that practically since the beginning of the government, the guaranty of the Fourth Amendment had been construed as recognizing a difference between a search of a store, dwelling house or other structure with respect to which a proper official warrant readily may be obtained, and a search of a ship, motorboat, wagon or automobile for contraband goods, where it is not practicable to secure a warrant because the vehicle can be quickly moved out of the locality or jurisdiction. With this qualification as to the right of search without a warrant, it was said that those lawfully within the country and entitled to use the public highways have a right to free passage without interruption or search, unless there is known to a competent official, authorized to search, probable cause for belief that their vehicles are carrying contraband or illegal merchandise. It was said further that the right to search and the validity of the seizure are not dependent upon the right to arrest, but on the reasonable cause of the civil officer for belief that the contents of the vehicle offend against the law. Probable cause exists "if the facts and circumstances before the officer are such as to warrant a man of prudence and caution in believing that the offense has been committed." [33]

Despite the safeguards which the Fifth and Sixth Amendments provided for the accused, and the observance of them, the conduct of the Federal Judges

[33] *Id.*, pp. 149, 153, 154, 158, 159, 161.

in criminal prosecutions at the very outset called forth severest condemnation. This was due to the rulings at Circuit that, in the absence of acts of Congress defining offenses, persons were subject to indictment and punishment under the English common law.[34] Able and conscientious judges took this view. The common law, it was said, was a part of our jurisprudence, and crimes must not go unpunished. Chief Justice Ellsworth developing this doctrine in a charge at Circuit, told the jury that it might indict for "acts manifestly subversive of the National Government, or of some of the powers specified in the Constitution." He said that it was not necessary that Congress should define the offense, but that "by the rules of a known law, matured by the reason of ages and which Americans have ever been tenacious of as a birthright, you will decide what acts are misdemeanours, on the ground of their opposing the existence of the National government or the efficient exercise of its legitimate powers."[35] This defiance of the American instinct of liberty caused a profound reaction. "The Common Law of England! May wholesome statutes soon root out this engine of oppression from America!"[36] was a popular toast of the Republicans at Boston. The Federal Judges added to their unpopularity by the manner in which they enforced the Sedition Law,[37]

[34] Beveridge's Marshall, Vol. III, pp. 23 *et seq.*
[35] Warren, *op. cit.*, Vol. I, p. 162.
[36] Beveridge, *op. cit.*, Vol. III, p. 24.
[37] 1 Statutes at Large, 596; Beveridge, *op. cit.*, Vol. III, p. 29.

and by their habit of making their charges to the
jury at Circuit the vehicle for political addresses.
What we have come to recognize as the appropriate
judicial demeanor was not an early tradition, and is
due more to the response which became necessary to
the public demand for complete impartiality in
judges, and for their aloofness from politics, than
to any magic effect of the wearing of the judicial
robe. The Supreme Court in 1812 decided that the
courts of the United States have no common law
jurisdiction in criminal cases. Justice Johnson gave
the opinion, saying, "Although this question is
brought up now for the first time to be decided by
this Court, we consider it as having been long since
settled in public opinion. * * * The legislative authority of the Union must first make an act a crime,
affix a punishment to it, and declare the Court that
shall have jurisdiction of the offense."[38] This was
said to be the opinion of the majority. Four years
later, a colloquy showed that the minority had not
yielded their views. Justice Story was still obdurate,
but the decision stood.[39]

The protection of the Fifth and Sixth Amendments
to persons accused of crime extends beyond the safeguards which would be included under the clause relating to due process of law. Thus, in the Federal
courts, in the case of a capital or otherwise infamous
crime, there must be a presentment or indictment of

[38] *United States v. Hudson*, 7 Cranch, 32.
[39] *United States v. Coolidge* (1816), 1 Wheaton, 415, 416.

a grand jury. This is not necessary in a State unless required by State law.[40] The requirement of due process under the Fourteenth Amendment does not make a trial by jury necessary in a State prosecution,[41] but there must be such a trial in criminal prosecutions in the Federal courts. The protection against compulsory self-incrimination guaranteed by the Fifth Amendment as against Federal action does not extend to State action, and the State is free, if it chooses by its Constitution and laws so to provide, to compel persons to be witnesses against themselves in a criminal prosecution.[42] The provision of the Federal Constitution as to jury trials extends under the Seventh Amendment to civil suits at common law in the Federal courts when more than twenty dollars are involved. The Supreme Court has gone so far as to hold that when a Circuit Court of Appeals found that there was not sufficient evidence to sustain a general verdict for the plaintiff, and that the trial court should have so instructed the jury, the appellate court could not, on the reversal of the judgment, direct in accordance with the State practice that judgment should be entered for the defendant but must award a new trial.[43]

It will be convenient to consider the due process clauses of the Fifth Amendment and Fourteenth

[40] *Hurtado v. California* (1884), 110 U. S. 516.

[41] *Maxwell v. Dow* (1900), 176 U. S. 581; *Tumey v. Ohio* (March 7, 1927).

[42] *Twining v. New Jersey* (1908), 211 U. S. 78.

[43] *Slocum v. New York Life Ins. Co.* (1913), 228 U. S. 364.

Amendment together as the language of both is substantially the same, — the one binding the Federal government and the other the States. But, before doing this, I may refer briefly to the decisions of the Supreme Court on some of the questions raised by the three amendments to the Federal Constitution which were adopted at the close of the Civil War. The Thirteenth Amendment provided that neither slavery nor involuntary servitude, except as a punishment for crime on due conviction, should exist within the United States or any place subject to their jurisdiction. This language reproduced the historic words of the Ordinance of 1787 for the government of the Northwest Territory. While the immediate concern was with African slavery, the Amendment was not limited to that. It was a charter of universal civil freedom for all persons, of whatever race, color or estate, under the flag. Involuntary servitude has a larger meaning than slavery. It was well understood that, in the form of apprenticeship for long terms, as it had been practiced in the West India Islands, on the abolition of slavery by the English government, or by reducing the slaves to the condition of serfs attached to the plantation, the purpose of the article might be evaded if only the word "slavery" were used.[44] Under the Amendment Congress properly prohibited peonage.[45] The plain intention was to render impossible

[44] *Slaughter House Cases* (1873), 16 Wallace, p. 69.

[45] Act of March 2, 1867, Chap. 187; 14 Statutes at Large, 546; U. S. Rev. Stat. Secs. 1990, 5526; *Clyatt v. United States* (1905), 197 U. S. 207.

any state of bondage, to make labor free, by prohibiting that control by which the personal service of one man is disposed of or coerced for another's benefit, which is the essence of involuntary servitude. In this view of the scope of the Amendment, a statute of Alabama was held to be invalid, by which refusal to work, where an employee had not repaid an advance of money, was made *prima facie* evidence of an intent to defraud and punishable as a criminal offense. The Act of Congress nullified State legislation which sought to compel service or labor by making it a crime to refuse or fail to perform it, as such laws would furnish the readiest means of compulsion. The exception in the Amendment as to punishment for crimes does not destroy the prohibition. The State may not compel a man to labor for another in payment of a debt.[46] An amusing instance of the perversity of the arguments sometimes addressed to the Court on constitutional questions was what the Supreme Court called "the rather singular ground" of a recent attack on provisions of the New York laws relating to apartment houses. It was contended by counsel that the law making it a misdemeanor for a landlord, or agent or janitor, intentionally to fail to furnish water, heat, light, elevator, telephone or other service which the lease required, constituted "involuntary servitude"![47]

The Fourteenth Amendment (Section 1) provides

[46] *Bailey v. Alabama* (1911), 219 U. S. 219.

[47] *Marcus Brown Holding Co. v. Feldman* (1921), 256 U. S. 170, 199.

that all persons born or naturalized in the United States, and subject to its jurisdiction, "are citizens of the United States and of the State wherein they reside." "No State shall make or enforce any law which shall abridge the privileges or immunities of citizens of the United States; * * *." Congress was empowered to enforce the provisions of the article by appropriate legislation. What was the effect of these solemn sentences written into the fundamental law as the outcome of civil war? Had they changed the structure of our government? There were not wanting opinions that they had. The argument was that a citizen of a State was now only a citizen of the United States residing in that State. The fundamental rights, privileges and immunities which belonged to him as a free man and a free citizen, now belonged to him as a citizen of the United States and were not dependent upon his citizenship of any State. The Amendment did not attempt to confer any new privileges or immunities upon citizens or to enumerate or define those already existing. It assumed that there were such privileges and immunities which belonged of right to citizens as such and ordained that they should not be abridged by State legislation. If this inhibition had no reference to privileges and immunities of this character, but only referred to such privileges and immunities as were before its adoption specially designated in the Constitution or necessarily implied as belonging to citizens of the United States, it was a vain and idle enactment, which accomplished nothing, and most unnecessarily excited Congress and the people on its passage. With the privileges and immunities thus designated no State could have ever interfered by its laws; the supremacy of the Constitution and the laws of the United States always had controlled State legislation of that character. But if the Amendment referred to the natural and inalienable rights which belonged to all citizens, the inhibition had a profound significance and consequence. Such was the contention.[48]

This fundamental question came before the Supreme Court in the *Slaughter House Cases*.[49] Louisiana had granted exclusive privileges for maintaining stock yards and slaughter houses and it was contended that the grant constituted an invasion of the private rights secured by the Amendment. There was a sharp division in the Court. Its opinion was delivered by one of the most eminent jurists who have adorned the bench, Justice Samuel F. Miller. All the members of the Court recognized the heavy responsibility involved. No questions so far-reaching and pervading in their consequences, so profoundly interesting to the people of the country, and so important in their bearing on the relations of the United States and of the several States to each other, and to the citizens of the States and of the United States, had come before them.[50] In constru-

---

[48] See dissenting opinion of Justice Field in the *Slaughter House Cases*, 16 Wallace, pp. 95, 96.

[49] (1873), 16 Wallace, 36.

[50] *Id.*, p. 67.

ing the Fourteenth Amendment, Justice Miller first observed that it declared that persons might be citizens of the United States without regard to their citizenship of a particular State. The Amendment overruled the *Dred Scott* decision by making all persons born within the United States and subject to its jurisdiction citizens of the United States. Then, it appeared that the Amendment recognized and established the distinction between citizenship of the United States and citizenship of a State. Under the clause in the Constitution [51] providing that the citizens of each State shall be entitled to all privileges and immunities of citizens in the several States, the question what were the privileges and immunities of citizens of the several States had already been answered. They were the fundamental rights belonging to the citizens of all free governments and which at all times had been enjoyed by citizens of the several States which compose the Union from the time of their becoming free, independent and sovereign. These rights embraced "nearly every civil right for the establishment and protection of which organized government is instituted." Justice Miller asked, Was it the purpose of the Fourteenth Amendment, by the simple declaration that no State should make or enforce any law which shall abridge the privileges and immunities of citizens of the United States, to transfer the security and protection of all these civil rights from the States to the Federal Government?

[51] Art. IV, Sec. 2.

And when it was declared that Congress should have the power to enforce that article, was it intended to bring within the power of Congress the entire domain of civil rights theretofore belonging exclusively to the States? The majority of the Court were convinced that no such result followed; that there was not so great a departure from the structure and spirit of our institutions as to subject the State governments to the control of Congress in the exercise of powers theretofore universally conceded to them of the most ordinary and fundamental character; and that the privileges and immunities which belonged to the citizen of the State as such were left to the State governments for security and protection and were not by this provision of the Fourteenth Amendment placed under the special care of the Federal Government.[52]

Four Justices dissented, Justices Field and Bradley in particular bringing their heaviest batteries to bear upon the prevailing opinion. Thirty years later, the Court observed that criticism of the decision in the *Slaughter House Cases* had never entirely ceased nor had the decision ever received universal assent by members of the Court. Undoubtedly it gave much less effect to the Fourteenth Amendment than some of the public men in framing it had intended, and disappointed many others. If, however, the views of the minority in that case had prevailed, it is easy to see how far the authority and independence of the

[52] 16 Wallace, pp. 73-79.

States would have been diminished by subjecting all their legislative and judicial acts to correction by the legislative, and review by the judicial, branch of the national government.[53] Unquestionably the Amendment caused citizenship of the United States to be paramount and dominant, instead of being subordinate and derivative.[54] But the distinction between National and State citizenship and their respective privileges and immunities has been firmly established.

"Privileges and immunities of citizens of the United States," Justice Moody said in *Twining* v. *New Jersey*, "are only such as arise out of the nature and essential character of the National Government, or are specifically granted or secured to all citizens or persons by the Constitution of the United States."[55] Thus, among the rights and privileges of national citizenship are the right to petition Congress for a redress of grievances; the right to vote for national officers; the right to enter the public lands; the right to be protected against violence while in the lawful custody of a United States marshal; the right to inform the United States authorities of violation of its laws.[56] Rights of this character are protected from abridgment by State action. A recent case illustrates the distinction. A provision

[53] *Twining v. New Jersey* (1908), 211 U. S. p. 96.
[54] *Selective Draft Law Cases* (1918), 245 U. S. 366, 389.
[55] (1908), 211 U. S. p. 97.
[56] *Id.*

of the criminal code of the United States makes it a crime to join in a conspiracy to oppress or intimidate a citizen in the free enjoyment of any right or privilege secured by the Constitution or laws of the United States.[57] Under this provision, there was an indictment in the Federal Court of Arizona for an alleged conspiracy against a large number of persons to deprive them of their right to remain peaceably within the State. The overt acts were the seizure and holding of these persons until they were forcibly transported into New Mexico and there released on threat of bodily harm should they ever return to Arizona. The fundamental right of citizens of the States which had existed from the beginning peacefully to dwell within the State, the right of free ingress and egress, was recognized. It had early been found to be one of the "privileges and immunities of citizens in the several States." This right, after the Fourteenth Amendment, continued to be left to the States for protection, and consequently the Supreme Court decided that individuals committing such acts as were the subject of complaint were appropriately punishable under State law and were not subject to Federal indictment, where there was no interference with the performance by the United States of its governmental functions.[58]

The Fifteenth Amendment provides that the right of citizens of the United States to vote shall not be

[57] U. S. Criminal Code, Sec. 19.
[58] *United States v. Wheeler* (1920), 254 U. S. 281.

denied or abridged by the United States or by any State on account of race, color or previous condition of servitude. The establishment of a literacy test may be regarded as the exercise by the State of a lawful power in determining the conditions of suffrage and is not subject to the supervision of the Federal courts in the absence of an unconstitutional discrimination. But such a test may be so connected with invalid tests as to make an entire statutory provision invalid. Thus, the so-called "grandfather's clause" of the amendment to the Constitution of Oklahoma was held to be void because of violation of the Fifteenth Amendment.[59] While the Fifteenth Amendment gave no right of suffrage, its command is self-executing, and rights of suffrage may be enjoyed by reason of the striking down of discriminations theretofore existing. The adoption of the Amendment had the effect, where State constitutions had conferred the right of suffrage on "all white male citizens" of causing the word "white" to disappear and all male citizens without discrimination on account of race, color or previous condition of servitude came under the generic grant of suffrage made by the State. The provision before the Court in the Oklahoma case imposed the suffrage test of ability to read and write any section of the Constitution of the State. It was all-inclusive, and contained no words of discrimination on account of race or color or any other reason, save that it was

[59] *Guinn v. United States* (1915), 238 U. S. 347.

immediately followed by the qualification: "but no person who was, on January 1, 1866, or at any time prior thereto, entitled to vote under any form of government, or who at that time resided in some foreign nation, and no lineal descendant of such person, shall be denied the right to register and vote because of his inability to so read and write sections of such constitution." The Supreme Court held that this was a discrimination made void by the Fifteenth Amendment because it was impossible to discover, unless the prohibitions of that Amendment were considered, the slightest reason for basing the classification upon a period of time prior to its adoption.[60] This decision was followed in a case involving the "grandfather's clause" in a Maryland statute fixing the qualifications of voters at municipal elections.[61] The opinions in both cases were delivered by Chief Justice White.

We may now turn to the due process clauses of the Fifth and Fourteenth Amendments; the one, limiting the exercise of power by the Federal Government; the other, aside from the questions raised by the "privileges and immunities" clause, subjecting to its restriction every repository of State power.[62] In each case, the prohibition is against deprivation "of life, liberty or property without due process of law." This phrase in the Fifth Amendment is the

[60] *Id.*, pp. 363-365.

[61] *Myers v. Anderson* (1915), 238 U. S. 368.

[62] *Home Telephone and Telegraph Co. v. Los Angeles* (1913), 227 U. S. 278, 286.

first use of it in an American constitution. It had appeared in an act of 1692 of the General Court of Massachusetts Bay.[63] Apparently it was first used in the statute of 28 Edward III.[64] Before the adoption of the Fifth Amendment, the declarations of rights during the period of the Revolution, beginning with the declaration of Virginia, had used the phrase of Magna Charta — "the law of the land," taken from the section which has been the citadel of liberty: "No free man shall be taken and imprisoned or disseized or exiled or in any way destroyed, nor. will we go upon him nor send upon him, except by the lawful judgment of his peers and by the law of the land." Before the Fifth Amendment, eight States of the thirteen had constitutional provisions referring to the "law of the land." This was the phrase of the Ordinance for the Northwest Territory. After the Fifth Amendment had become a part of the Federal Constitution, the phrase "due process of law" came gradually into use in State constitutions, New York being the first to adopt the exact words in the second constitution of 1821. With very few exceptions, it is now found in all the State constitutions. There have been differences in wording in the course of the evolution of constitutional provisions, but without difference in substance; the phrase "due process of law" represents an American conception of extraordinary pervasiveness.

[63] Act of October 12, 1692, Art. 5; "Acts and Resolves of the Province of Massachusetts Bay," Vol. I, Chap. 11, Art. 5, p. 40.

[64] Statutes at Large of Gr. Br. & Ireland, Vol. I, p. 643.

It has been said by eminent legal historians of England that it was possible for men to worship the words of Magna Charta, because it was possible to misunderstand them, and yet it was recognized that "with all its faults this document becomes and rightly becomes a sacred text, the nearest approach to an irrepealable, fundamental statute, that England has ever had." [65] On this side of the water, the words of Magna Charta may have been misunderstood, but the spirit of Magna Charta dominated political thought. The Colonists invoked the "rights of Englishmen." They had a notion of rights that were fundamental, immutable, and they intended to make these rights secure. It matters not whether they were accurate in their understanding of the Great Charter, for the point is not what it meant when granted by King John, but what the Colonists thought it meant, and what the framers and ratifiers of our constitutional provisions intended by "law of the land" or "due process of law." They did not attempt to define the meaning of the phrase; doubtless it appeared to them as having an indefinite content, and it was all the better for that. They wanted protection against tyranny, wherever and however it might hit, and they were not careful even to try to limit by exact definition the guaranty of their liberties. It would be easy to show that the requirements of proper procedure in criminal cases, and in civil

[65] Pollock and Maitland, *History of English Law,* Vol. 1, p. 152.

cases also, had large place in their minds. But it would be going too far to insist that these requirements were all they had in view. They were also intent on safeguards against arbitrary government. They were intent on protection against legislatures as well as executives. Madison probably drafted the Fifth Amendment, and it was Madison, as I have already noted, who said that the judicial tribunals would be, in a peculiar sense, the guardians of the rights safeguarded by the amendments and would be "an impenetrable bulwark against every assumption of power in the Legislative or Executive." [66] But if legislative encroachments were thus to be guarded against, was the guaranty against such encroachments limited to changes in matters of procedure? If the legislature was not to be permitted by any law to dispense with the essentials of a just course of judicial procedure, was the legislature none the less to be free to enact laws which would operate to deprive one of life, liberty or property by an arbitrary fiat? It would be difficult to maintain such a hypothesis, and at the same time to do justice to the temper and dominant thought of the builders of our constitutions. If they cherished a desire to resist both legislative and executive arbitrariness, they would naturally wish to have a guaranty of security in flexible terms. They preferred flexibility to certainty. The phrase "due process of law" was vague, its meaning was unsettled, but it was not mean-

[66] See *supra,* page 160, note 7.

ingless nor was it limited by anything short of the general purpose to afford immunity from any violation of fundamental rights.

The question is not an open one in American courts, and it is not my purpose to review the historical argument but to give some idea of the work of the Supreme Court in providing a content for this clause and in establishing a standard for judicial action in its application.   Until the Court was called upon to deal with the due process clause of the Fourteenth Amendment in relation to State action, the Court had but little occasion to consider its purport. Webster in his argument in the *Dartmouth College Case* [67] made the classic statement: "By the law of the land is most clearly intended the general law; a law, which hears before it condemns; which proceeds upon inquiry, and renders judgment only after trial. The meaning is, that every citizen shall hold his life, liberty, property, and immunities under the protection of the general rules which govern society. Everything which may pass under the form of an enactment, is not, therefore, to be considered the law of the land.   If this were so, acts of attainder, bills of pains and penalties, acts of confiscation, acts reversing judgments, and acts directly transferring one man's estate to another, legislative judgments, decrees, and forfeitures, in all possible forms, would be the law of the land."   At about the same time, it had been remarked by the Court that these words in the Constitution of Maryland "were intended to .secure

[67] (1819), 4 Wheaton, 518, 581, 582.

the individual from the arbitrary exercise of the powers of government, unrestrained by the established principles of private rights and distributive justice.'' [68] But it was more than fifty years after the adoption of the Fifth Amendment that the Supreme Court had presented to it a case of Federal action requiring the interpretation of the due process clause. Justice Curtis, speaking for the Court, gave this interpretation, the question being raised as to distress warrants issued by the Solicitor of the Treasury under an Act of 1820.[69] ''The words, 'due process of law,' were undoubtedly intended to convey the same meaning as the words, 'by the law of the land,' in *Magna Charta*. Lord Coke in his commentary on those words, (2 Inst. 50) says they mean due process of law. * * * That the warrant now in question is legal process, is not denied. It was issued in conformity with an act of Congress. But is it 'due process of law'? The constitution contains no description of these processes which it was intended to allow or forbid. It does not even declare what principles are to be applied to ascertain whether it be due process. It is manifest that it was not left to the legislative power to enact any process which might be devised. The article is a restraint on the legislative as well as on the executive and judicial powers of the government, and cannot be so construed as to leave congress free to make any process 'due process of law' by its mere will. To what principles, then,

[68] *Bank of Columbia v. Okely* (1819), 4 Wheaton, 235, 244.
[69] Act of May 15, 1820, c. 107, 3 Statutes at Large, 592.

are we to resort to ascertain whether this process enacted by congress is due process? To this the answer must be twofold. We must examine the constitution itself, to see whether this process be in conflict with any of its provisions. If not found to be so, we must look to those settled usages and modes of proceeding existing in the common and statute law of England, before the emigration of our ancestors, and which are shown not to have been unsuited to their civil and political condition by having been acted on by them after the settlement of this country." [70]

When the Fourteenth Amendment was proposed and adopted, it seems that there was but little discussion of the due process clause, and the wide scope of the Federal jurisdiction it authorized was not appreciated. The question was presented in the *Slaughter House Cases,* but was dismissed with a brief statement.[71] In 1878, the Court through Justice Miller,[72] after referring to the history of the clause, observed "that the constitutional meaning or value of the phrase 'due process of law' remains today without that satisfactory precision of definition which judicial decisions have given to nearly all the other guaranties of personal rights found in the constitutions of the several States and of the United States. It is easy to see that when the great barons of England wrung from King John, at the point of

[70] *Murray's Lessee v. Hoboken Land and Improvement Co.* (1855), 18 Howard, 272, 276, 277.

[71] (1873), 16 Wallace, p. 80.

[72] *Davidson v. New Orleans,* 96 U. S. 97, 101, 102.

the sword, the concession that neither their lives nor their property should be disposed of by the crown, except as provided by the law of the land, they meant by 'law of the land' the ancient and customary laws of the English people, or laws enacted by the Parliament of which those barons were a controlling element. It was not in their minds, therefore, to protect themselves against the enactment of laws by the Parliament of England. But when, in the year of grace 1866, there is placed in the Constitution of the United States a declaration that 'no State shall deprive any person of life, liberty, or property without due process of law,' can a State make anything due process of law which, by its own legislation, it chooses to declare such? To affirm this is to hold that the prohibition to the States is of no avail, or has no application where the invasion of private rights is effected under the forms of State legislation. It seems to us that a statute which declares in terms, and without more, that the full and exclusive title of a described piece of land, which is now in A, shall be and is hereby vested in B, would, if effectual, deprive A of his property without due process of law, within the meaning of the constitutional provision." In the great number of cases which even at that time, had been presented to the Supreme Court attacking State legislation under this clause, Justice Miller found abundant evidence "that there exists some strange misconception" of the scope of the provision. "In fact, it would seem," said he, "from the character of many of the cases before us, and the arguments made in them, that the clause under consideration is looked upon as a means of bringing to the test of the decision of this court the abstract opinions of every unsuccessful litigant in a State court of the justice of the decision against him, and of the merits of the legislation on which such a decision may be founded. If, therefore, it were possible to define what it is for a State to deprive a person of life, liberty or property without due process of law, in terms which would cover every exercise of power thus forbidden to the State, and exclude those which are not, no more useful construction could be furnished by this or any other court to any part of the fundamental law. But, apart from the imminent risk of failure to give any definition which would be at once perspicuous, comprehensive, and satisfactory, there is wisdom, we think, in the ascertaining of the intent and application of such an important phrase of the Federal Constitution, by the gradual process of judicial inclusion and exclusion, as the cases presented for decision shall require, with the reasoning on which such decisions may be founded. This court is, after an experience of nearly a century, still engaged in defining the obligation of contracts, the regulation of commerce, and other powers conferred on the Federal government, or limitations imposed upon the States.'' [73]

Six years later in relation to the question, to which I have already adverted, as to the necessity of an indictment in a State criminal prosecution for murder

[73] *Id.*, p. 104.

in order to afford due process, the Supreme Court through Justice Stanley Matthews [74] drew the distinction that while a process of law, not otherwise forbidden, should be taken to be due process of law if it could show the sanction of settled usage both in England and this country, it did not follow that nothing else could be sustained as due process. That, said he, "would be to deny every quality of the law but its age, and to render it incapable of progress or improvement. It would be to stamp upon our jurisprudence the unchangeableness attributed to the laws of the Medes and the Persians." This would be, he thought, all the more singular and surprising in this quick and active age when we consider "that owing to the progressive development of legal ideas and institutions in England, the words of Magna Charta stood for very different things at the time of the separation of the American colonies, from what they represented originally." Justice Matthews summed up his conclusions in these memorable words: "The Constitution of the United States was ordained, it is true, by descendants of Englishmen, who inherited the traditions of English law and history; but it was made for an undefined and expanding future, and for a people gathered and to be gathered from many nations and of many tongues. And while we take just pride in the principles and institutions of the common law, we are not to forget that in lands where other systems of jurisprudence prevail, the ideas and processes of civil justice are also

[74] *Hurtado v. California* (1884), 110 U. S. 516, 528, 529.

not unknown. Due process of law, in spite of the absolutism of continental governments, is not alien to that code which survived the Roman Empire as the foundation of modern civilization in Europe, and which has given us that fundamental maxim of distributive justice — *suum cuique tribuere*. There is nothing in Magna Charta, rightly construed as a broad charter of public right and law, which ought to exclude the best ideas of all systems and of every age; and as it was the characteristic principle of the common law to draw its inspiration from every fountain of justice, we are not to assume that the sources of its supply have been exhausted. On the contrary, we should expect that the new and various experiences of our own situation and system will mould and shape it into new and not less useful forms." [75] In that case the Supreme Court recognized that our written constitutions were deemed essential to protect the rights and liberties of the people against encroachments of power delegated to their governments and that the provisions of the bills of rights "were limitations upon all the powers of government, legislative as well as executive and judicial. * * * Applied in England only as guards against executive usurpation and tyranny, here they have become bulwarks also against arbitrary legislation; but, in that application, as it would be incongruous to measure and restrict them by the ancient customary English law, they must be held to guarantee not particular forms of procedure, but the very

[75] *Id.*, p. 531.

substance of individual rights to life, liberty, and property.'' [76]

What is this substance? This is the question which the Supreme Court is daily called upon to answer, as case after case presents the never ending invocation of the Fourteenth Amendment. No one has a vested right in the common law. Both Congress and the State legislatures must have a wide field of legislative discretion that is essential to the exercise of legislative power. The due process clause does not substitute the judgment of the Court for this discretion of the legislature. The legislative action may be unwise without being arbitrary to the point of transcending the limits of its authority. Its action may be economically unsound without being constitutionally invalid. Even as to procedure, the legislature is not bound to provide an ideal system. Changing social conditions require new remedies, the novel exercise of the police power, to care for both social and individual interests. Our Federal Constitution has vested in the Supreme Court, and the inferior Federal courts, the judicial, not the legislative, power. Those who find fault with the multiplicity of laws, and with vexatious interferences, normally must address themselves to the legislature, and not to the courts; they have their remedy at the ballot box.

But there is a limit. To take familiar illustrations — no one would contend that the legislature could take A's property and give it to B, or enact a law

[76] *Id.*, pp. 531, 532.

that no one under six feet in height should be allowed to sell groceries. It would naturally be said that constitutional provisions are not needed to protect against such legislative extravagances. But the point is that the framers of the Constitution were not content to take their chance with legislative omnipotence, and while such extreme measures might not be expected, there was reason for apprehension that there would be encroachments, likewise indefensible, because capricious and of an entirely arbitrary character. And thus the duty rests upon the Supreme Court which it cannot escape, to apply this test to legislation. It is not surprising that there are many close cases which divide the Court, and that legislative action which seems to some members of the Court to be wholly arbitrary appears to others to fall within the legislative competency. Some decisions under the due process clause have evoked the most violent criticism as inconsistent with the standards of judicial action and as betraying a lack of appreciation of social needs. What is more remarkable is the broad range of cases in which legislative action, to an extent which in an earlier period would have been deemed to be unjustified, has been sustained and the manifest reluctance of the Court to assert judicial authority against the legislative will. A recent illustration will show its methods of reasoning in dealing with new situations. I refer to the decision as to the validity of a zoning ordinance in an Ohio village, a suburb of Cleveland.[77] Justice Sutherland, delivering the opinion of the Court said: "Building zone laws are of modern origin. They began in this country about twenty-five years ago. Until recent years, urban life was comparatively simple; but with the great increase and concentration of population, problems have developed, and constantly are developing, which require, and will continue to require, additional restrictions in respect of the use and occupation of private lands in urban communities. Regulations, the wisdom, necessity and validity of which, as applied to existing conditions, are so apparent that they are now uniformly sustained, a century ago, or even half a century ago, probably would have been rejected as arbitrary and repressive. Such regulations are sustained, under the complex conditions of our day, for reasons analogous to those which justify traffic regulations, which, before the advent of automobiles and rapid transit street railways, would have been condemned as fatally arbitrary and unreasonable. And in this there is no inconsistency, for while the meaning of constitutional guaranties never varies, the scope of their application must expand or contract to meet the new and different conditions which are constantly coming within the field of their operation. In a changing world, it is impossible that it should be otherwise. But although a degree of elasticity is thus imparted, not to the *meaning*, but to the *appli-*

[77] *Euclid v. Ambler County* (1926), 272 U. S. 365.

*cation* of constitutional principles, statutes and ordinances, which, after giving due weight to the new conditions, are found clearly not to conform to the Constitution, of course, must fall. * * * A regulatory zoning ordinance, which would be clearly valid as applied to the great cities, might be clearly invalid as applied to rural communities. * * * Thus the question whether the power to forbid the erection of a building of a particular kind or for a particular use, like the question whether a particular thing is a nuisance, is to be determined, not by an abstract consideration of the building or of the thing considered apart, but by considering it in connection with the circumstances and the locality. * * * A nuisance may be merely a right thing in the wrong place, — like a pig in the parlor instead of the barnyard. If the validity of the legislative classification for zoning purposes be fairly debatable, the legislative judgment must be allowed to control." [78] On reviewing all the circumstances, and the reasons for the zoning ordinance in question, the Court added that if these reasons did "not demonstrate the wisdom or sound policy in all respects" of the restrictions, "the reasons are sufficiently cogent to preclude us from saying, as it must be said before the ordinance can be declared unconstitutional, that such provisions are clearly arbitrary and unreasonable, having no substantial relation to the public health, safety, morals or general welfare." And the Court again

[78] *Id.*, pp. 386-388.

set forth its traditional policy that in the realm of constitutional law "it has perceived the embarrassment which is likely to result from an attempt to formulate rules or decide questions beyond the necessities of the immediate issue. It has preferred to follow the method of a gradual approach to the general by a systematically guarded application and extension of constitutional principles to particular cases," and this process applies with peculiar force "to the solution of questions arising under the due process clause of the Constitution as applied to the exercise of the flexible powers of police." [79]

[79] *Id.*, pp. 395, 397.

## VI

## Liberty, Property and Social Justice (*Continued*)

The Constitution prohibited both Congress and the States from passing bills of attainder and *ex post facto* laws.[1] A bill of attainder is a legislative act which inflicts punishment without a judicial trial; in such a case, the legislature assumes judicial magistracy.[2] The prohibition of *ex post facto* laws relates only to criminal proceedings and includes such legislation as by its necessary operation, and in relation to the offense or its consequences, alters the situation of the accused to his disadvantage. To bring a statute under this interdiction, it is not enough merely to change modes of procedure but the statute must materially affect the right of the accused to have his guilt determined by the law as it was when the offense was committed.[3] The requirements of due process, under the Fifth and Fourteenth Amendments make it necessary that legislation looking to the future, and creating new offenses, shall establish an ascertainable standard of guilt and suitably inform accused persons of the nature and cause of the accusation. The *Lever Act* passed

[1] Art. I, Sec. 9, par. 3; Art. I, Sec. 10, par. 1.

[2] *Cummings v. Missouri* (1867) 4 Wallace, 277, 323.

[3] *Thompson v. Utah* (1898), 170 U. S. 343, 351.

by Congress in 1917, and amended in 1919,[4] which made it a crime to charge an unjust or unreasonable rate, or to conspire to exact excessive prices, was altogether too indefinite to be valid under the Fifth and Sixth Amendments, and these constitutional provisions were applied to the statute notwithstanding the existence of a state of war.[5] The Act left open the widest conceivable inquiry, the result of which no one could foreshadow or adequately guard against.

The Constitution, prior to the Amendments, denied to the States the power to pass laws impairing the obligation of contracts.[6] This prohibition refers to the exertion of legislative power and does not extend to mere errors in the decisions of the State courts.[7] It does, however, embrace the legislative action taken by subordinate bodies, as, for example, municipal ordinances passed under the authority of the legislature.[8] In the *Dartmouth College Case* the charter of the college was held to be a contract which could not be altered by New Hampshire in a material respect without the consent of the college.[9] The ef-

[4] Act of August 10, 1917, c. 53, 40 Statutes at Large 276; Act of October 22, 1919, c. 80, 41 Statutes at Large, 297.

[5] *United States v. Cohen Grocery Co.* (1921), 255 U. S. 81; *Weeds, Inc. v. United States* (1921), 255 U. S. 109.

[6] Art. I, Sec. 10, par. 1.

[7] *Cross Lake Shooting & Fishing Club v. Louisiana* (1912), 224 U. S. 632.

[8] *Grand Trunk Western R'w'y Co. v. South Bend* (1913), 227 U. S. 544.

[9] *Dartmouth College v. Woodward* (1819), 4 Wheaton, 518.

fect of this decision has been obviated to a large extent by the reservations made by the States, in granting charters or permitting incorporation under general laws, of the right of amendment or repeal. In the absence of such a reservation, the doctrine holds good and has frequently been applied to corporate franchises. But it is also to be observed that special franchises which are granted in order that they may be exercised for the public benefit carry with them the implied condition that they may be lost by misuser or nonuser.[10] Charter grants are also strictly construed against the grantees as was decided by the Supreme Court in an opinion by Chief Justice Taney in the *Charles River Bridge Case*.[11] On such a construction, although a company had erected at great expense a toll bridge over the Charles River, it was held that there being no exclusive privilege expressly granted, it had no constitutional ground for objecting to the construction of a second bridge close by. In a letter written by Justice Story to Charles Sumner,[12] we have an interesting description of the arguments in this celebrated case and a glimpse of the scene in the Supreme Court when the case was heard. Justice Story said: "Our friend Greenleaf's argument was excellent — full of ability, point, learning, condensed thought, and

[10] *New York Electric Lines Co. v. Empire City Subway Co.* (1914), 235 U. S. 179, 194.

[11] *Charles River Bridge v. Warren Bridge* (1837), 11 Peters, 420.

[12] W. W. Story, *Life and Letters of Joseph Story*, Vol. II, p. 266; Warren, *op. cit.* Vol. II, p. 297.

strong illustration, — delivered with great presence of mind, modestly, calmly, and resolutely. * * * at the same time, I do not say that he will win the cause. That is uncertain yet, and will not probably be decided under weeks to come. I say so the more resolutely because on some points he did not convince me; but I felt the force of his argument. * * * Webster's closing reply was in his best manner, but with a little too much of *fierté* here and there. * * * The audience was very large, especially as the cause advanced; — a large circle of ladies, of the highest fashion, and taste, and intelligence, numerous lawyers, and gentlemen of both houses of Congress, and towards the close, the foreign ministers, or at least some two or three of them.'' I doubt if in recent years judges of the Supreme Court have indulged in such intimate descriptions while cases are under consideration. Justice Story was greatly disturbed by Chief Justice Taney's opinion and dissented vigorously. He wrote to Justice McLean: ''There will not, I fear, ever in our day, be any case in which a law of a State or of Congress will be declared unconstitutional; for the old constitutional doctrines are fast fading away, and a change has come over the public mind, from which I augur little good.'' [13]

Congress, unlike the States, is not prohibited from passing laws impairing the obligation of contracts. But in so far as contract rights have attached, and may be regarded as property, the due

[13] Story, *op. cit.* Vol. II, p. 272; Warren, *op. cit.* Vol. II, p. 302.

process clause of the Fifth Amendment protects them from direct impairment. This was stated in the first legal tender decision.[14] But this does not mean that when the Constitution gives an express power to Congress, it may not be exercised although its exertion may interfere with the operation of contracts previously made. Prior arrangements are necessarily subject to this paramount authority. Thus, bankruptcy laws, regulations of interstate commerce, the exercise of the war power, may destroy the worth of contracts without giving ground for objection under the Constitution.

The extent to which the States, aside from the prohibition against impairing the obligation of past contracts, may go in forbidding the making of future contracts, is involved in the general question as to the scope of the guaranty of liberty. Liberty embraces much more than immunity from physical restraint, or from criminal prosecutions in the absence of a prior valid definition of the offense, a proper charge, due notice and a reasonable opportunity to defend. The liberty guaranteed by the Constitution, includes, as the Supreme Court has said,[15] the right of a person "to be free in the enjoyment of all his faculties; to be free to use them in all lawful ways; to live and work where he will; to earn his livelihood by any lawful calling; to pursue any livelihood or avocation, and for that purpose to

[14] *Hepburn v. Griswold* (1870), 8 Wallace, p. 624.
[15] *Allgeyer v. Louisiana* (1897), 165 U. S. 578, 589.

enter into all contracts'' which may be appropriate for the carrying out of these purposes. But this freedom is manifestly a qualified and not an absolute right. There can be no absolute freedom in civilized society to do as one wills or to contract as one chooses.[16] As Justice Holmes has observed, ''pretty much all law consists in forbidding men to do some things that they want to do, and contract is no more exempt from law than other acts.''[17] Liberty implies the absence of arbitrary restraint, not immunity from reasonable regulations or prohibitions imposed in the interest of the community. The State may establish qualifications for the practice of law or medicine, or for any vocation requiring particular training or skill for the protection of the public. It is within the power of government to restrain some individuals from all contracts, as well as all individuals from some contracts. Thus it may deny to all the right to contract for the purchase or sale of lottery tickets; to the minor the right to assume any obligations except for the necessaries of existence; to the common carrier, the power to make any contract releasing himself from negligence.[18] The right to make contracts is subject, as already noted, to the exercise of the powers granted to Congress for the conduct of matters of national concern. In 1871, one

[16] *Chicago, B & Q. R. R. Co. v. McGuire* (1911), 219 U. S. 549, 567.

[17] Dissenting opinion in *Adkins v. Children's Hospital* (1923), 261 U. S. p. 568.

[18] *Frisbie v. United States* (1895), 157 U. S. p. 165.

Mottley settled his claim for injuries received through the negligence of a railroad, and as a part of the agreement he and his wife were to have free passes on the railroad as long as they lived. This arrangement, however, could not stand against the action of Congress when the Hepburn Act of 1906 prohibited free passes.[19] In the field of State action, liberty to contract is subject to the essential authority of government to maintain peace and security, and to enact laws for the promotion of the well-being of those subject to its jurisdiction, that is, in the exercise of what we call the police power. Usury and Sunday laws are an historic example. It was under this authority that the Supreme Court sustained the validity of State legislation in prohibiting (prior to the Eighteenth Amendment) the manufacture and sale of intoxicating liquors within the State;[20] in prohibiting the sale of cigarettes without license,[21] in requiring the redemption in cash of store orders or other evidences of indebtedness issued in payment of wages;[22] in making it unlawful to contract for options to sell or buy grain or other commodity at a future time;[23] in limiting the hours of work of women in specified employments;[24] in limiting the hours of

[19] *Louisville & Nashville R. R. Co. v. Mottley* (1911), 219 U. S. 467.

[20] *Mugler v. Kansas* (1887), 123 U. S. 623.

[21] *Gundling v. Chicago* (1900), 177 U. S. 183.

[22] *Knoxville Iron Co. v. Harbison* (1901), 183 U. S. 13.

[23] *Booth v. Illinois* (1902), 184 U. S. 425.

[24] *Muller v. Oregon* (1908), 208 U. S. 412; *Riley v. Massachusetts* (1914), 232 U. S. 671; *Miller v. Wilson* (1915), 236 U. S. 373.

men employed in manufacturing establishments;[25] in requiring employers of miners to pay for coal by weight before screening;[26] in controlling the use of trading stamps and redeemable coupons in connection with sales of merchandise;[27] in forbidding payment of sailors in advance;[28] in fixing the size of a loaf of bread;[29] in providing workmen's compensation, covering compensation for injuries caused without the fault of the employer.[30] These are illustrations of the wide range of the decisions of the Supreme Court sustaining the power to restrict the liberty of contract, and to these might be added a host of regulations upheld in the interest of health, safety, morals and public welfare, against the operation of which no contract would be permitted to stand.

There have been decisions, dealing with this extremely difficult question of the scope of the constitutional guaranty of liberty, which have evoked the strong protest of members of the Court and much public criticism. The case of this sort which perhaps more than any other has been the object of attack is that of *Lochner* v. *New York*,[31] decided a little over

[25] *Bunting v. Oregon* (1917), 243 U. S. 426. See *Holden v. Hardy* (1898), 169 U. S. 366.

[26] *McLean v. Arkansas* (1909), 211 U. S. 539.

[27] *Rast v. Van Deman & Lewis Co.* (1916), 240 U. S. 342.

[28] *Patterson v. Bark Eudora* (1903), 190 U. S. 169.

[29] *Schmidinger v. Chicago* (1913), 226 U. S. 578.

[30] *New York Central R. R. Co. v. White* (1917), 243 U. S. 188; *Arizona Employers' Liability Cases* (1919), 250 U. S. 400.

[31] (1905) 198 U. S. 45.

twenty years ago, where the Court held that a statute limiting employment in bakeries to ten hours a day was an arbitrary interference with liberty of contract. The opinion was by Justice Peckham and went upon the ground that, while the statute would have been valid beyond question if enacted in the interest of health, it was not in truth a health law. There were four dissents, by Justices Harlan, White, Day and Holmes. The differentiations which may appeal to the judicial judgment in this class of cases are illustrated by the fact that Justice Harlan, who was vigorous in dissent in the *Lochner* case and gave many instances of the extent of the valid exercise of the police power,[32] delivered the opinion of the Court in the case of *Adair*.[33] There it was decided that personal liberty as well as the right of property was invaded without due process of law by the Act of Congress [34] which made it a criminal offense for an agent of an interstate carrier to discharge an employee because of his membership in a labor organization. It was also decided that there was no such relation to interstate commerce as to sustain the Act under the commerce clause. The Court placed the right of the employer to discharge, for whatever reason, on the same footing as the right of the employee to quit, for whatever reason. On similar grounds, a statute of Kansas was held to be invalid

[32] *Id.*, pp. 65-74.
[33] *Adair v. United States* (1908), 208 U. S. 161.
[34] Act of June 1, 1898, c. 370, 30 Statutes at Large, 424.

which made it a crime to prescribe as a condition of
the employment, that the employee should agree not
to become or remain a member of a labor organization during his employment.[35] But Justice Pitney,
who gave the opinion for the Court in that case,
wrote a few years later for the majority of the
Court in sustaining a statute of Missouri which required an employing corporation to furnish to an
employee, who was discharged or voluntarily quit, a
letter setting forth the nature and duration of the
service and the cause, if any, of the employee's
leaving it.[36] This was regarded as a regulation of
corporations. Recently, the Supreme Court decided [37] against the validity of the Act of Congress [38]
providing for the fixing of a minimum wage for
women and children in the District of Columbia.
The majority of the Court, by Justice Sutherland
(who has since written the opinion of the Court sustaining the zoning ordinance, to which I referred at
the close of the last lecture) said that the feature of
the statute which, perhaps more than any other, in
the Court's opinion, put upon it the stamp of invalidity was that it exacted from the employer "an
arbitrary payment for a purpose and upon a basis
having no causal connection with his business, or the
contract or the work the employee engages to do." [39]

[35] *Coppage v. Kansas* (1915), 236 U. S. 1.
[36] *Prudential Insurance Co. v. Cheek* (1922), 259 U. S. 530.
[37] *Adkins v. Children's Hospital* (1923), 261 U. S. 525.
[38] Act of September 19, 1918, c. 174, 40 Statutes at Large, 960.
[39] 261 U. S. p. 558.

The Court said that the act did not deal with any business charged with a public interest or with public work or was not to meet and tide over a temporary emergency; it had nothing to do with the character, methods or periods of wage payments; it did not prescribe hours of labor or conditions under which labor was to be done; it was confined to adult women who were legally as capable of contracting for themselves as men.[40] The Chief Justice and Justices Holmes and Sanford dissented. Justice Brandeis did not sit. The Chief Justice, without expressing an opinion that a minimum wage limitation could be enacted for adult men, thought that it could be applied to women. He believed that the legislature could find as much support in experience for the view that a sweating wage had as great and as direct a tendency to bring about an injury to the health and morals of workers as long hours of labor had to injure health.[41] He found no reason for the conclusion that the Nineteenth Amendment, although it gave to women political power, had changed their physical strength or limitations, or deprived the legislature of the right to take these differences into account.[42] It was in his dissenting opinion in this case that Justice Holmes observed that the earlier decisions upon the due process clause of the Fourteenth Amendment "began within our memory and went no farther than an unpretentious assertion of

[40] *Id.,* p. 554.
[41] *Id.,* p. 566.
[42] *Id.,* p. 567.

the liberty to follow the ordinary callings. Later that innocuous generality was expanded into the dogma, Liberty of Contract." He thought that among the restrictive laws that had been upheld there were those that interfered with liberty of contract quite as seriously and directly as the one then before the Court.[43]

The Chief Justice, shortly after, spoke for a unanimous Court in holding that the general freedom of employer and employee to contract with respect to wages was protected by the due process clause. That was in a case involving the validity of the statute of Kansas establishing a Court of Industrial Relations.[44] This was an attempt to compel those engaged in the manufacture of food and clothing, and the production of fuel, whether owners or workers, to continue in their business and employment on terms fixed by an agency of the State, if they could not agree. The statute gave the Industrial Court authority to permit the owner or employer to go out of the business, if he showed that he could only continue, on the terms fixed, at such heavy loss that collapse would follow, but this privilege was generally illusory. A laborer dissatisfied with his wages was permitted to quit, but he might not agree with his fellows to quit or combine with others to induce them to quit. The Act was held to be invalid under the due process clause as an unwarrantable deprivation of property and liberty of contract. It was con-

[43] *Id.*, p. 568.
[44] *Wolff Packing Co. v. Industrial Court* (1923), 262 U. S. 522.

sidered "as compelling the employer to pay the adjudged wages, and as forbidding the employees to combine against working and receiving them." "Without this joint compulsion, the whole theory and purpose of the act would fail." If limitations of continuity upon the employer and the employed could ever be justified, it must be, said the Court, "where the obligation to the public of continuous service is direct, clear and mandatory and arises as a contractual condition express or implied of entering the business either as owner or worker. It can only arise when investment by the owner and entering the employment by the worker create a conventional relation to the public somewhat equivalent to the appointment of officers and the enlistment of soldiers and sailors in military service." [45]

Again, however, the differences between the Justices in their points of view appeared in the decision holding invalid a statute of Nebraska which prescribed the weights of loaves of bread.[46] In the opinion of the Court, delivered by Justice Butler, it was recognized as beyond doubt that the police power of the State might be exercised to protect purchasers from imposition by the sale of short weight loaves. The particular provisions of the statute under consideration were found to be arbitrary. Justices Brandeis and Holmes dissented in an elaborate opinion. Many years ago a law of Pennsylvania which

[45] *Id.*, p. 541.
[46] *Burns Baking Co. v. Bryan* (1924), 264 U. S. 504.

prohibited the manufacture, sale, or possession for sale of oleomargarine was sustained.[47] But in a recent case [48] it was decided (Justices Holmes, Brandeis and Stone dissenting) that a statute of Pennsylvania forbidding the use, in comfortables, of shoddy, even when sterilized, violated the due process clause of the Fourteenth Amendment. The distinction was stated to be that in the earlier case it had been assumed that most kinds of oleomargarine were or might become injurious to health, but that in the case before the Court it was established that sterilization eliminated the dangers if any from the use of shoddy and hence the act could not be sustained as a health measure. It was also found that it could not be upheld as preventing deception. The Court decided that the business involved was legitimate and useful, and that the attempted regulation was "purely arbitrary." [49]

State action in another relation has furnished the occasion for the Supreme Court to apply the restraints found in the due process clause to interferences with the freedom of learning, or at least to the freedom of teachers, and of parents to engage teachers to instruct their children. In 1919, Nebraska enacted a law prohibiting any person to teach any subject in a private, denominational, parochial or public school in any other than the English language.

[47] *Powell v. Pennsylvania* (1888), 127 U. S. 678.

[48] *Weaver v. Palmer Brothers Co.* (1926), 270 U. S. 402.

[49] *Id.*, p. 415. See also, *Fairmont Creamery Co. v. Minnesota* (April 11, 1927).

Other languages could be taught only after the pupil had passed the eighth grade. The Supreme Court set aside a conviction, which the State court had sustained, for teaching the German language in a Lutheran parochial school.[50] Justices Holmes and Sutherland dissented.[51] The Court, through Justice McReynolds, said that the guaranty of liberty embraced the right of the individual "to engage in any of the common occupations of life, to acquire useful knowledge, to marry, establish a home and bring up children, to worship God according to the dictates of his own conscience, and generally to enjoy those privileges long recognized at common law as essential to the orderly pursuit of happiness by free men." The calling of teachers was useful and honorable, — essential, indeed, to the public welfare. Mere knowledge of the German language could not reasonably be regarded as harmful. The accused had taught this language as part of his occupation. "His right thus to teach and the right of parents to engage him so to instruct their children," were "within the liberty of the Amendment." It was remarked that some of the plans which had been suggested for the improvement of society were not available under our Constitution. "For the welfare of his Ideal Commonwealth," said Justice McReynolds, "Plato suggested a law which should provide: 'That the wives of our guardians are to be common, and their children are

[50] *Meyer v. Nebraska* (1923), 262 U. S. 390; see also, *Bartels* v. *Iowa* (1923), 262 U. S. 404.

[51] *Id.*, pp. 403, 412.

to be common, and no parent is to know his own child, nor any child his parent. * * * The proper officers will take the offspring of the good parents to the pen or fold, and there they will deposit them with certain nurses who dwell in a separate quarter; but the offspring of the inferior, or of the better when they chance to be deformed, will be put away in some mysterious, unknown place, as they should be.' In order to submerge the individual and develop ideal citizens, Sparta assembled the males at seven into barracks and intrusted their subsequent education and training to official guardians. Although such measures have been deliberately approved by men of great genius, their ideas touching the relation between individual and State were wholly different from those upon which our institutions rest; and it hardly will be affirmed that any legislature could impose such restrictions upon the people of a State without doing violence to both letter and spirit of the Constitution.'' [52] This decision was followed by the *Oregon School* case.[53] There, the statute had been adopted under the initiative provision of the State constitution. It required every parent, guardian or other person having control of a child between the ages of eight and sixteen years to send him ''to a public school'' for the period of time a public school was held during the current year in the district where the child resided. No question was raised concerning the power of the State reasonably

[52] *Meyer v. Nebraska*, 262 U. S. pp. 400-402.
[53] *Pierce v. Society of Sisters* (1925), 268 U. S. 510.

to regulate all schools or to require that all children of proper age attend some school. The inevitable practical result of enforcing the statute would be destruction of the primary schools of those who invoked the jurisdiction of the court. It was decided that the act unreasonably interfered with the liberty of parents and guardians to direct the upbringing and education of children under their control.

In dealing with questions arising under the due process clause of the Fourteenth Amendment, the Supreme Court early recognized the authority of the legislature to regulate a business, and the use of property, when it is "clothed with a public interest." In the celebrated case of *Munn* v. *Illinois* [54] the Court decided, Chief Justice Waite giving the opinion, that the State could fix the maximum of charges for the storage of grain in warehouses. The principle was established as far back as the time of Lord Chief Justice Hale who said that when private property is affected with a public interest it ceases to be *juris privati* only. "When therefore," said the Court in the *Munn* case, "one devotes his property to a use in which the public has an interest, he in effect grants to the public an interest in that use, and must submit to be controlled by the public for the common good to the extent of the interest he has thus created. He may withdraw his grant by discontinuing the use; but so long as he maintains the use, he must submit to the control." "We know," it was added, "that this is a power which may be

[54] (1876) 94 U. S. 113.

abused" but "for protection against abuses by legislatures the people must resort to the polls not to the
courts." [55] In another case,[56] heard at the same time,
an Illinois statute fixing maximum railroad rates
was sustained and Chief Justice Waite observed
with respect to the system of classification adopted
in the exercise of the legislative discretion: "Our
province is only to determine whether it could be
done at all, and under any circumstances. If it
could, the legislature must decide for itself, subject
to no control from us, whether the common good requires that it should be done." [57] Justice Field dissented in these cases, but he had already said with
respect to the regulation of the sale of intoxicating
liquors that "no one has ever pretended, that I am
aware of, that the fourteenth amendment interferes
in any respect with the police power of the State,"[58]
and this view he reasserted in delivering the opinion
of the Court in a later case.[59] But it is apparent that
the difference between holding that the Fourteenth
Amendment did not restrict the police power but that
legislative acts could be found to be invalid which
lay outside that power, and determining that the
police power was limited by the Amendment to the
extent that injurious legislation which was arbitrary
and capricious was prohibited, is not a difference of
much practical value. Observations, such as that

[55] *Id.,* pp. 126, 134.
[56] *Chicago, B. & Q. R. R. Co. v. Iowa* (1876), 94 U. S. 155.
[57] *Id.,* p. 164.
[58] *Bartemeyer v. Iowa* (1873), 18 Wallace, 129, 138.
[59] *Barbier v. Connolly* (1885), 113 U. S. 27, 31.

of Justice Field, were taken to mean that the Amendment did not interfere with the *proper* exercise of the police power. The doctrine of the absolute control of the legislature over railroad rates could not stand, if the principle of protection against arbitrary legislation was to be maintained. The due process clause of the Fourteenth Amendment, despite the repeated refusals of the Court to find that the guaranty had been violated, was constantly invoked as a refuge from the increasing volume and variety of legislation burdening rights of property. In 1885, Chief Justice Waite spoke for the Court in sustaining Mississippi in establishing a railroad commission with power to fix rates.[60] But the opinion contained this sentence: "This power to regulate is not a power to destroy, and limitation is not the equivalent of confiscation. Under pretence of regulating fares and freights, the State cannot require a railroad corporation to carry persons or property without reward; nor can it do that which in law amounts to a taking of private property without just compensation, or without due process of law."[61] This was the assertion of jurisdiction, which has ever since been exercised, to review the action taken by the legislature or under its authority in fixing the charges of public service corporations, for the purpose of determining whether the action is confiscatory, an inquiry which has given rise to the most intricate and perplexing questions that come before ju-

[60] *Railroad Commission Cases* (1886), 116 U. S. 307.
[61] *Id.*, p. 331.

dicial tribunals. In 1890, the Supreme Court decided that a Minnesota law which (as interpreted by the State Court) allowed a railroad commission to fix rates which were final, and forbade the courts to stay the hands of the commission although the rates might be unequal and unreasonable, was invalid.[62] Justice Bradley, with whom Justices Gray and L. Q. C. Lamar concurred, said that in his view the final arbitrament lay with the legislature and not with the judiciary.[63] Four years later the Supreme Court sustained a decree enjoining the Commission of Texas from enforcing rates found to be unjust and unreasonable.[64] In 1898, Justice Harlan delivered the opinion of the Court in *Smyth* v. *Ames*[65] holding that rates fixed by a Nebraska statute were confiscatory. The question was there presented as to the method of determining whether rates were confiscatory and it was laid down that the basis of all calculations must be "the fair value" of the property being used by the company for the convenience of the public; upon this value the company was entitled to a fair return. It is worthy of note that Mr. William J. Bryan appeared for the Board of Transportation of Nebraska in this case and contended that the present value of the roads, as measured by the cost of reproduction, should be taken as the basis of calculation.[66]

[62] *Chicago, M. & St. P. R'w'y Co.* v. *Minnesota,* 134 U. S. 418.
[63] *Id.,* p. 462.
[64] *Reagan v. Farmers' Loan & Trust Co.,* 154 U. S. 362.
[65] 169 U. S. 466.
[66] *Id.,* p. 489.

This was to get rid of watered stock and fictitious capitalization. In recent years, when cost of reproduction has mounted so high, there has been an effort, as yet unsuccessful, to establish what is called "the prudent investment value" as the basis of determining the fair value.[67] The Supreme Court has said that the ascertainment of fair value is not controlled by artificial rules. It is not a matter of formulas, but there must be a reasonable judgment having its basis in a proper consideration of all relevant facts.[68] This involves, under the rule of *Smyth* v. *Ames*, a very broad inquiry. But, in applying these principles, it is recognized that the rate-making power is a legislative power and necessarily implies a range of legislative discretion. The Court does not sit as a board of revision to substitute its judgment for that of the legislature, or of a commission lawfully constituted by it, as to matters within the province of either. The question is whether the State has overstepped constitutional limits by making rates so unreasonably low that they must be regarded as confiscatory.

There could be no question but that railroads, and what are called public utilities, are clothed with a public interest, but what other undertakings are within this category? It was decided, against the strong dissenting opinion of Justice J. R. Lamar,

[67] See dissenting opinion of Brandeis J., in *Southwestern Bell Telephone Co.* v. *Public Service Commission* (1923), 262 U. S. 276, 289; *McCardle* v. *Indianapolis Water Co.* (1926), 272 U. S. 400.

[68] *Minnesota Rate Cases* (1913), 230 U. S. p. 434.

that the insurance business was included so as to justify the regulation of rates.[69] In the case of the Kansas Industrial Relations Court, already mentioned, Chief Justice Taft thus stated the result of the decisions: "Businesses said to be clothed with a public interest justifying some public regulation may be divided into three classes: (1) Those which are carried on under the authority of a public grant of privileges which either expressly or impliedly imposes the affirmative duty of rendering a public service demanded by any member of the public. Such are the railroads, other common carriers and public utilities. (2) Certain occupations, regarded as exceptional, the public interest attaching to which, recognized from earliest times, has survived the period of arbitrary laws by Parliament or Colonial legislatures for regulating all trades and callings. Such are those of the keepers of inns, cabs and grist mills. * * * (3) Businesses which, though not public at their inception may be fairly said to have risen to be such and have become subject in consequence to some government regulation. They have come to hold such a peculiar relation to the public that this is superimposed upon them. * * * the mere declaration by a legislature that a business is affected with a public interest is not conclusive of the question whether its attempted regulation on that ground is justified. The circumstances of its alleged change from the status of a private business

[69] *German Alliance Insurance Co. v. Lewis* (1914), 233 U. S. 389, 418.

and its freedom from regulation into one in which the public have come to have an interest are always a subject of judicial inquiry. * * * It has never been supposed, since the adoption of the Constitution, that the business of the butcher, or the baker, the tailor, the wood chopper, the mining operator or the miner was clothed with such a public interest that the price of his product or his wages could be fixed by State regulation. It is true that in the days of the early common law an omnipotent Parliament did regulate prices and wages as it chose, and occasionally a Colonial legislature sought to exercise the same power; but nowadays one does not devote one's property or business to the public use or clothe it with a public interest merely because one makes commodities for, and sells to, the public in the common callings of which those above mentioned are instances." [70]

The Supreme Court has recognized that the legislature may meet public emergencies by action that ordinarily would go beyond its constitutional authority. This principle is not limited to military exigencies in the theater of war, or to the extraordinary requirements of some great public calamity. Less grave, but unusual and urgent conditions, may just-

[70] *Wolff Packing Co. v. Industrial Court* (1923), 262 U. S. pp. 535-537. Since the delivery of this lecture, the Supreme Court has decided that places of amusement or entertainment are not public utilities or so affected with a public interest as to justify legislative regulation of the charges which their patrons may be required to pay. *Tyson & Brother v. United Theatre Ticket Officers*, (February 28, 1927).

ify temporary expedients. Thus, the Supreme Court sustained the action of Congress for the relief of tenants in the District of Columbia because of a notorious situation growing out of the World War,[71] and at the same time the Court upheld the New York law of 1920 suspending under specified conditions the right of landlords to recover possession of their property.[72] The Court said in the former case that "the space in Washington is necessarily monopolized in comparatively few hands, and letting portions of it is as much a business as any other. Housing is a necessary of life." [73] The Chief Justice and Justices McKenna, Van Devanter and McReynolds dissented. In 1917, the Supreme Court sustained the Adamson Act prescribing wages for railroad employees; it was passed to prevent a strike of railroad trainmen.[74] Chief Justice Taft later observed that this decision, although it concerned an interstate carrier in the presence of a nation-wide emergency, and the possibility of a great disaster, went to the border line, and nothing was found in that case which justified the sort of regulation sought by the statute establishing the Kansas Industrial Relations Court.[75]

The due process clause does not prevent the creation of administrative bodies which act as legislative agencies in order to apply reasonable legislative

[71] *Block v. Hirsh* (1921), 256 U. S. 134.
[72] *Marcus Brown Holding Co. v. Feldman* (1921), 256 U. S. 170
[73] 256 U. S. p. 156.
[74] *Wilson v. New*, 243 U. S. 332, 342.
[75] 262 U. S. pp. 541, 542, 544.

standards to the fact of particular cases. Findings of fact, made by such bodies on evidence, may be final. But administrative orders, quasi-judicial in character, as was said by Justice J. R. Lamar in speaking for the Court, are void if a hearing is denied, or if that granted is inadequate or manifestly unfair, or if the finding is contrary to the indisputable character of the evidence, or if the facts found do not as matter of law support the order. A finding in such cases without evidence "is arbitrary and baseless." [76]

Closely related to the due process clause is the one forbidding the taking of private property for public use without just compensation. This prohibition, explicit in the Fifth Amendment, is deemed to be embraced in the due process clause of the Fourteenth Amendment.[77] And, in considering property rights, it must always be remembered that the community can carry out its public purposes if it is willing to pay. What is a public purpose is a judicial question and cannot be foreclosed by legislative declarations. But the courts give to the opinion of the legislature the greatest deference short of admitting its controlling character. Thus, the condemnation of a right of way across a placer mining claim for the aerial bucket line of a mining corporation was held not to be invalid as a taking of private property for private use, as the legislature and the

[76] *Interstate Commerce Commission v. Louisville & Nashville R. R. Co.* (1913), 227 U. S. 88, 91.

[77] *Chicago, B. & Q. R. R. Co. v. Chicago* (1897), 166 U. S. 266.

highest court of Utah had said that the public welfare of that State demanded aerial lines between the mines upon its mountain sides.[78] A similar principle is applied when the State exercises its taxing power. Every presumption in its favor is indulged and "only clear and demonstrated usurpation of power will authorize judicial interference." This was said in a case where the power of North Dakota to lay taxes to carry out such enterprises as a State bank, a State warehouse, elevator and flour mill system, and a State home building project, was challenged and sustained.[79] The respect for the legislative judgment is illustrated in many cases arising under the due process clause. When, for example, the legislature acts for the protection of the public health, it is not enough that the subject of its action should be regarded as debatable. "If it be debatable, the legislature is entitled to its own judgment," and that is not to be superseded by the verdict of a jury or by the personal opinion of judges on the issue which the legislature had decided.[80]

The Fourteenth Amendment not only requires due process but prohibits a State from denying to any person the equal protection of the laws. This provision, and that of the due process clause, are "universal in their application, to all persons within the territorial jurisdiction, without regard to any differences in race, of color, or of nationality; and the

[78] *Strickley v. Highland Boy Mining Co.* (1906), 200 U. S. 527.
[79] *Green v. Frazier* (1920), 253 U. S. 233, 239.
[80] *Price v. Illinois* (1915), 238 U. S. 446, 452.

equal protection of the laws is a pledge of the protection of equal laws."[81] It was applied in the leading case of *Yick Wo*[82] in the holding that the administration of a municipal ordinance of San Francisco which made an arbitrary and unjust discrimination, founded on differences in race between persons otherwise in similar circumstances, violated the constitutional provision. The following statement of Justice Stanley Matthews, in the opinion in that case, is probably as frequently quoted in the Supreme Court as any deliverance from the bench: "Though the law itself be fair on its face and impartial in appearance, yet, if it is applied and administered by public authority with an evil eye and an unequal hand, so as practically to make unjust and illegal discriminations between persons in similar circumstances, material to their rights, the denial of equal justice is still within the prohibition of the Constitution."[83] Another illustration is found in a statute of Arizona which provided that an employer of more than five workers at any one time, regardless of kind or class of work, or sex of workers, should employ not less than eighty per cent. qualified electors or native born citizens of the United States or some subdivision thereof; it was held to be invalid.[84] The constitutional right in that case was successfully invoked by a cook, a native of Austria, who was discharged because his

[81] *Yick Wo v. Hopkins* (1886), 118 U. S. 356, 369.
[82] *Id.*
[83] *Id.*, pp. 373, 374.
[84] *Truax v. Raich* (1915), 239 U. S. 33.

employer had nine employees of whom seven were neither native born citizens nor qualified electors. The most striking fact, however, in the application of the equal protection clause is the recognition of the wide range of classification which is incident to the legislative power of the State. Almost daily, in the Supreme Court, counsel appeal to this clause but without avail because of this right of classification, which it must appear has been abused by clearly arbitrary action before the Court will pronounce a State statute invalid. Dealing with practical exigencies, the legislature may be guided by experience. It is free to recognize degrees of harm, and it may confine its restrictions to those classes of cases where the need is deemed to be clearest. It may proceed cautiously, step by step, and if an evil is specially experienced in a particular branch of business it is not necessary that the prohibition should be couched in all-embracing terms.[85]

The distinction between "due process" and "equal protection" has been pointed out by Chief Justice Taft:[86] "It may be that they overlap, that a violation of one may involve at times the violation of the other, but the spheres of the protection they offer are not coterminous. The due process clause, brought down from Magna Charta, was found in the early state constitutions and later in the Fifth Amendment to the Federal Constitution as a limitation upon the

[85] *Carroll v. Greenwich Insurance Co.* (1905), 199 U. S. 401 411.
[86] *Truax v. Corrigan* (1921), 257 U. S. 312, 332, 333.

executive, legislative and judicial powers of the Federal Government, while the equality clause does not appear in the Fifth Amendment and so does not apply to congressional legislation. The due process clause * * * of course, tends to secure equality of law in the sense that it makes a required minimum of protection for every one's right of life, liberty and property, which the Congress or the legislature may not withhold. * * * But the framers and adopters of this Amendment'' (the Fourteenth) ''were not content to depend on a mere minimum secured by the due process clause, or upon the spirit of equality which might not be insisted on by local public opinion. They therefore embodied that spirit in a specific guaranty. The guaranty was aimed at undue favor and individual or class privilege, on the one hand, and at hostile discrimination or the oppression of inequality on the other. It sought an equality of treatment of all persons, even though all enjoyed the protection of due process.'' This statement was made in a case which arose out of a dispute between the plaintiffs who were employers and the defendants' union which had ordered a strike. In the conduct of the strike the Court found that there were libelous attacks upon the plaintiffs, their business, their employees and their customers, which were uttered in aid of the plan to induce customers to withhold their patronage; there were picketing with banners announcing the plaintiffs' unfairness and threats of injurious consequences to future customers, and other wrongful conduct, all linked together in a campaign "constituting an unlawful annoyance and a hurtful nuisance in respect of the free access to the plaintiffs' place of business. It was not lawful persuasion or inducing. It was not a mere appeal to the sympathetic aid of would-be customers by a simple statement of the fact of the strike and a request to withhold patronage. It was compelling every customer or would-be customer to run the gauntlet of most uncomfortable publicity, aggressive and annoying importunity, libelous attacks and fear of injurious consequences, illegally inflicted, to his reputation and standing in the community. * * * Violence could not have been more effective."[87] In a situation of that sort, it was held that a State law which, as construed by the State court, specially exempted ex-employees when committing wrongful and irreparable injury to the business of their former employer, from restraint by injunction, while leaving subject to such restraint all others engaged in like wrong-doing, was unreasonable and invalid. Justices Holmes, Pitney, Clark, and Brandeis dissented.[88]

The labors of the Supreme Court in applying general clauses of an undefined content are not limited to the duty of giving effect to the Constitution. The Court is the final interpreter of the acts of Congress. Statutes come to the judicial test not simply of con-

[87] *Id.,* pp. 327, 328.
[88] *Id.,* pp. 342-376.

stitutional validity but with respect to their true import, and a federal statute finally means what the Court says it means. The English language has always been found to be a difficult medium for exactness in law making; hence, there is much legal verbiage, where a business man would naively use a simple phrase although, if put to a crucial test, it might reveal several different meanings of which he was happily unconscious. The legislature, in search of an elusive definiteness, often resorts to needless verbal complications which must be disentangled by the courts to get at the legislature's intent; not, of course, an intent outside, but one which must be found inside, the words used. What is worse is that not infrequently the passage of a measure is assured only through the compromises found in general clauses which mean different things to different minds, and the courts are left to resolve what the legislature should have clarified and thus to bear the criticism of those who desired to have the statute in the form the legislature would not adopt. The more important the subject, the more probable is this emulation in statutory clauses of constitutional indefiniteness. We have a conspicuous illustration of this in the Sherman Anti-Trust Act of 1890,[89] prohibiting every contract and combination or conspiracy in restraint of trade or commerce among the several States or with foreign nations. The act was saved from invalidity on the score of complete uncertainty because of its use of an historic phrase

[89] Act of July 2, 1890, c. 647, 26 Statutes at Large, 209.

which could be deemed to set up a legal standard,[90] although it is safe to say no business man knew what it was, or for that matter, after thirty years of interpretation can even now be sure as to what he can lawfully do although he has been advised as to much which is forbidden. It is manifest that if the Anti-Trust Act had received a literal interpretation and had been regarded as condemning all contracts which might produce any restraint of interstate trade, it would have hopelessly tied up our commercial activities, and most appropriate business relations would have become impossible if an act so interpreted could have been upheld as constitutional. It would not do to construe the statute so as to inhibit, for example, an ordinary contract of partnership, or of employment, between two persons previously engaged in the same line of business, the purchase by one' wholesale merchant of the product of two producers, the sale of the good will of a business with an agreement not to destroy its value by engaging in a similar enterprise. But if all acts which would have the effect of imposing some restraint on interstate commerce were not prohibited, what was to be the test? The Supreme Court in the *Standard Oil* and *Tobacco* cases [91] decided that only such contracts and combinations are within the Act as by reason of intent or the inherent nature of the

[90] *Nash v. United States* (1913), 229 U. S. 373, 377; *United States v. Addyston Pipe & Steel Co.*, 85 Fed. Rep. 271, s.c. 175 U. S. 211; see *Cline v. Frink Dairy Co.* (May 31, 1927).

[91] *Standard Oil Co. v. United States* (1911), 221 U. S. 1; *American Tobacco Co. v. United States* (1911), 221 U. S. 106.

contemplated acts prejudice the public interest by unduly restricting competition or unduly obstructing the course of trade.[92] The Court has said: "In the absence of a purpose to monopolize or the compulsion that results from contract or agreement, the individual certainly may exercise great freedom; but concerted action through combination presents a wholly different problem and is forbidden when the necessary tendency is to destroy the kind of competition to which the public has long looked for protection." [93] "Any concerted action by any combination of men or corporations to cause, or which in fact does cause direct, undue restraint of competition in such (interstate) commerce falls within the condemnation of the act." [94] The facts of each case must be examined in the light of these general principles, in order to determine whether there is an undue restraint. Under this burden of endeavoring to anticipate the judgment of the courts, large business transactions have been conducted for a generation: Despite the uncertainty, there can be no doubt of the general salutary effect of the legislation, but it shows quite clearly that even in the field of the exercise of its power Congress voluntarily leaves much to the courts.

[92] *Nash v. United States* (1913), 229 U. S. p. 376.

[93] *United States v. American Linseed Oil Co.* (1923), 262 U. S. 371, 390. If it is found that there is an agreement to fix prices, it falls under the condemnation of the statute, although the prices agreed upon are reasonable and the parties acted with good intentions. *United States v. Trenton Potteries Co.* (February 21, 1927.)

[94] *American Column Co. v. United States* (1912), 257 U. S. 377, 400.

Questions in relation to the activities of trade associations have frequently been presented, and the extent to which the Court has gone in upholding reasonable freedom is shown by recent decisions. Where all the manufacturers of hand-blown window glass had established a wage scale which was issued to one set of factories for one period, and to another for a second period, but no factory could get it for both, the agreement was enjoined in the lower court. But the Supreme Court found that there were not men enough in the industry to enable the factories to run continuously during the working season and that the purpose of the arrangement was to secure employment for all of the men during the whole of two seasons and thus to give all the labor available to the factories and to divide it equally among them.[95] There was no unreasonable restraint of trade in that. In two recent cases relating to trade associations Justice Stone, delivering the opinion of the Court, reviewed the decisions.[96] Referring to the activities of trade associations in distributing information he said: "We realize that such information, gathered and disseminated among the members of a trade or business, may be the basis of agreement or concerted action to lessen production arbitrarily or to raise prices beyond the levels of production and price which would prevail if no such agreement or

[95] *National Association of Window Glass Manufacturers v. United States* (1923), 263 U. S. 403.

[96] *Maple Flooring Manufacturers Association v. United States* (1925), 268 U. S. 563; *Cement Manufacturers Protective Association v. United States* (1925), 268 U. S. 588.

concerted action ensued and those engaged in commerce were left free to base individual initiative on their information of the essential elements of their business. Such concerted action constitutes a restraint of commerce and is illegal and may be enjoined.'' But it was decided that trade associations ''which openly and fairly gather and disseminate information as to the cost of their product, the volume of production, the actual price which the product has brought in past transactions, stocks of merchandise on hand, approximate cost of transportation from the principal points of shipment to the points of consumption,'' and whose members ''meet and discuss such information and statistics without however reaching or attempting to reach any agreement or any concerted action with respect to prices or production or restraining competition, do not thereby engage in unlawful restraint of commerce.'' [97]

The Supreme Court has held that unincorporated labor unions are suable in their own names in the Federal courts for violation of the Anti-Trust Act and that the funds accumulated by them to be expended in conducting strikes are subject to execution in suits for torts committed by such unions in strikes.[98] But it must be remembered that production — coal mining, for example — is not interstate commerce and the power of Congress does not ex-

[97] 268 U. S. pp. 585, 586.

[98] *United Mine Workers of America v. Coronado Coal Co.* (1922), 259 U. S. 344.

tend to its regulation as such. So it has been decided that obstruction to coal mining is not necessarily a direct obstruction to interstate commerce in coal.[99] But when the intent of those unlawfully preventing the manufacture or production of a commodity is shown to be to restrain or control the supply entering into and moving in interstate commerce, or the price of it in interstate commerce, the Supreme Court decided, in an opinion by Chief Justice Taft, that their action was a direct violation of the Anti-Trust Act.[100]

I have shown these cross-sections of the jurisprudence of the Supreme Court in order that you may see the grain and growth of the tree. It has been impossible, of course, to be comprehensive or to give you a critique. Anything approaching adequacy in the discussion of constitutional questions, or a criticism of a host of decisions, would require a treatise. But enough has been said, I hope, to interpret to you the work of the Court, its method, its general principles, — the way in which the judges approach and perform their task. I have endeavored to indicate the highest levels of judicial work, and to give you, in their own language although by brief excerpts, the points of view of our most illustrious

[99] *Id.*, pp. 407, 408.

[100] *Coronado Coal Co. v. United Mine Workers of America* (1925), 268 U. S. 295, 310.

jurists. The Court has thus, I trust, been permitted fairly to interpret itself.

Much of the criticism of the Court deals with what is occasional rather than typical. In looking to the future the fundamental questions are these: Are we ready to give up a written constitution with its definition of powers? Do we desire to abandon our dual system and to confer upon a single legislature the supreme authority of the people through a completely centralized government? If we maintain our dual system and a written constitution, with the limitations essential to such a plan, do we wish to attempt to define more specifically in the Constitution the division of authority as, for example, in relation to interstate commerce? Is it likely that we could make a success of such a plan? If we prefer to retain the dual system and limited governmental powers, are we ready to give to Congress the final determination whether the States exceed the powers retained by them or whether Congress transcends the limitations of its own powers? If not, what substitute is there to suggest for the Supreme Court? Do we desire constitutional questions, if such there are to be, to be determined by political assemblies and by partisan divisions? Is there any better plan, whatever imperfections our present one may have, for securing a reasonably continuous, non-partisan and philosophical exposition of the Constitution than by regarding it as the supreme law of the land to be applied in actual cases and controversies through the

exercise of the judicial power? These are the questions which must be considered in discussing the
value of the work of the Supreme Court, which in a
practical and systematic way enables us to draw
upon our resources of reason in maintaining the
balance of rights which is characteristic of the Republic.

Proposals for changes in the organization and the
exercise of the jurisdiction of the Supreme Court
have been of two sorts; those suggested for the purpose of promoting its efficiency and those which have
been sought to curb the exertion of the judicial power. Relief from the laborious duty at Circuit became
absolutely necessary if the Justices were properly
to attend to the work of the Supreme Court. The
establishment of Circuit Courts of Appeals, as intermediate appellate tribunals, was a most important improvement in the Federal judicial system. It
has been said that "perhaps the decisive factor in
the history of the Supreme Court is its progressive
contraction of jurisdiction." [101] But the limitation
of the scope of review, as a matter of right on the
part of litigants, has been accompanied by the pres-
ervation of the judicial authority to review in the
cases deemed appropriate for its exercise. The selection of such cases, in an increasing degree, has
been left with the Supreme Court itself. Efforts
further to increase the number of judges have failed.
After the number of associate justices had been en-

[101] *Harvard Law Review*, Vol. 39, p. 1046.

larged to eight in 1837, Justice Story wrote: "You may ask how the Judges got along together? We made very slow progress, and did less in the same time than I ever knew. The addition to our numbers has most sensibly affected our facility as well as rapidity of doing business. 'Many men of many minds' require a great deal of discussion to compel them to come to definite results; and we found ourselves often involved in long and very tedious debates. I verily believe, if there were twelve Judges, we should do no business at all, or at least very little." [102] Doubtless, a rhetorical exaggeration to emphasize a strong point! Everyone who has worked in a group knows the necessity of limiting size to obtain efficiency. And this is peculiarly true of a judicial body. It is too much to say that the Supreme Court could not do its work if two more members were added, but I think that the consensus of competent opinion is that it is now large enough. Happily, suggestions for an increased number and for two divisions of the Court have not been favored because of their impracticality in view of the character of the Court's most important function.

A certain plausibility has attached to the proposal that legislation should not be held to be unconstitutional by a bare majority of the judges, but that the concurrence of six, or even of seven, judges should be required. Difficulties at once suggest themselves If, for example, a lower Federal Court, or a State

[102] Story, *op. cit.* Vol. 2, p. 296; Warren, *op. cit.* Vol. II, p. 316.

Court has held legislation to be unconstitutional, is the decision to be reversed by a minority of the Supreme Court who believe it to be constitutional? It is often said, when a decision of the Court is by a vote of five to four, that one judge determines the result. This is more striking than accurate, for the actual decision is that of five judges. But if the concurrence of six judges were required, then if there were four judges of the opinion that the statute was constitutional they would in effect out-vote the five and it could still be said that the vote of one judge had made the result possible, as otherwise there might have been the required six votes. If seven votes were necessary to hold a statute invalid, then three judges would outweigh six on a judicial question, and still a change of one vote might be determinative.

It is urged that as legislation should be held to be repugnant to the Constitution only in clear cases, and as this is recognized as a principle of decision, a division in the Court should be regarded as enough to show reasonable doubt. Plainly, that suggestion cannot be carried to its logical limit. If it were, the action of a single judge in the court of first instance, holding an act to be constitutional would be conclusive, for is he not a reasonable man? Or, if that judge decided the act to be unconstitutional, and in the Circuit Court of Appeals two judges agreed with him, but the third dissented, should not the majority bow to his dissent as sufficiently indicating doubt?

We have similar considerations with respect to State court decisions. Why have any review by the Supreme Court in such cases, unless the courts under review, whether Federal or State, should hold legislation to be unconstitutional? And, then, on the view suggested, their unanimous opinions to this effect might be overthrown, and the legislation still be sustained, if a minority of the Supreme Court considered it to be valid, as a vote of the majority of the Supreme Court would not be sufficient to render a contrary decision.

In truth, judges will have their convictions, and it is of the essence of the appropriate exercise of judicial power that these should be independently expressed. Divisions on close questions cannot be prevented. The unpopularity of a decision against the constitutionality of a legislative act is sometimes too readily assumed by those who propose changes. It has already been observed that our history shows serious complaint in certain important cases where acts of Congress have been sustained. If the object is to create public content with the result, it would not likely be obtained if a statute highly obnoxious to many, as interfering with cherished liberty of action, were made effective by a minority of the highest court. It must also be remembered that we are considering the exercise of the judicial power which the Constitution places in one Supreme Court and the lower Federal courts. The Supreme Court has appellate jurisdiction with such

exceptions and under such regulations as are made
by Congress. But making allowance for such exceptions and giving effect to such regulations as Congress may appropriately provide with respect to the
cases in which the appellate jurisdiction shall be exercised, when the appellate jurisdiction attaches to a
case the judicial power extends to it, and it is doubtful to say the least if Congress would have the constitutional authority to fetter the exercise of the
judicial power by giving the control of it to the
minority of the Court. In a small group, the action
of any one may be of decisive effect, no matter what
rule may be adopted, and the method that best accords with our traditions and is most likely to have
public favor in the long run is that of decision by the
majority.

In our system, the individual finds security in his
rights because he is entitled to the protection of tribunals that represent the capacity of the community
for impartial judgment as free as possible from the
passion of the moment and the demands of interest
or prejudice. The ends of social justice are achiev-
ed through a process by which every step is examined in the light of the principles which are our in-
heritance as a free people. The spirit of the work
of the Supreme Court permeates every legislative
assembly and every important discussion of reforms
by legislative action. We largely subject our political thinking to the conception of law, not as an arbitrary edict of power, but as governed by the funda-

mental conceptions of justice. No one is above the law. The officer of government, the State itself, is subject to the fundamental law that the humblest may invoke. Our relations to each other, to the society of which we are a part, to the governments, Federal and State, which are the organs of that society, come to the judicial test, as far removed from the intrusions of artifice, selfishness and caprice as any test can be. The Supreme Court is the embodiment of this conception of our law, the exemplar of its application, and the assurance that in the complexities of an extraordinarily expanded life, we have not forgotten the ancient faith by which we have pledged ourselves to render to each one his due, — a faith which alone makes it possible to look to the coming years with confidence as well as hope.

(THE END)

# TABLE OF CASES CITED

## A

## B

# INDEX

**Date Due**

| | | | | |
|---|---|---|---|---|
| | | | | |
| | | | | |
| | | | | |
| | | | | |
| | | | | |
| | | | | |
| | | | | |
| | | | | |
| | | | | |
| | | | | |
| | | | | |
| | | | | |
| | | | | |